CICI or CLARISSA McNAIR was born in Mississippi, and graduated from Briarcliff College in New York. In Toronto, she worked as a researcher for CBC-TV's award-winning documentary on organized crime called *Connections*. In Rome, she was a news writer, newscaster, and producer of documentaries for Vatican Radio. She was also the weekend news anchor for WROM-TV. In Los Angeles, she worked in film.

McNair has published several novels, a memoir, and has written about true crime. As a private detective, her cases include missing persons, intellectual property, stolen art recovery, blackmail, rape, and murder. She is a foreign correspondent with World Radio Paris; McNair writes and produces *Basic Black*, vignettes of crime, scandal, and death, which is broadcast in Paris.

BOOKS BY CICI McNAIR

Detectives Don't Wear Seat Belts
Never Flirt with a Femme Fatale
Kiss the Risk

BOOKS BY CLARISSA McNAIR

Garden of Tigers
A Flash of Diamonds
Dancing With Thieves
The Hole in the Edge

Praise for Cici McNair's *Detectives Don't Wear Seat Belts:*

"A wonderful, wonderful read, an amazing true story told in the voice of a born storyteller . . . she's funny, she's honest and completely fascinating . . . This is a memoir written by someone who made her own life into an adventure story, and who knows exactly how to grab your hand and pull you along."

—Perri Klass, author of *The Mercy Rule*

"This improper Southern belle's memoir as a private detective combines the immediate impact of a newspaper column with the ironic detachment of a fine novel. McNair's crafted vignettes of low-rent detectives are like chocolate truffles: dark, bittersweet and addictive."

—Bruce Schimmel, founder and columnist, *Philadelphia City Paper*

"Detectives may not wear seat belts, but you definitely should hang on to your seat when you read Cici McNair's saucy, smart memoir about a hot female P.I. from the South. I always knew Cici was a pistol, but she really blew me away with this one!"

—Lewis Burke Frumkes,
author of *How to Raise Your I.Q. by Eating Gifted Children*

"Cici McNair is the most glammapuss lady detective since Nora Charles . . ."

—Phoebe Eaton, novelist and screenwriter

Praise for *Never Flirt with a Femme Fatale:*

"A classic from the hands of a pro . . . what makes this book work so well is that the author is part of the drama. Besides being a fine and skilled writer, she is a Private Investigator."

—John W. Bowers, associate professor, Columbia University,
and author of *Love in Tennessee*

"Real life drama told with a master storyteller's touch. If you like Dominick Dunne then you will love *Never Flirt with a Femme Fatale.*"

—Donna Huston Murray,
author of The Ginger Barnes Main Line Murder mysteries

MURDER,
ACTUALLY

Vignettes of a Private Detective

CICI McNAIR, P.I.

FEDORA PRESS

Handwritten inscription:

March 2019

To Mary Ellen and Jim —

all the mysteries actually

Cici

so many thanks for the very good work. It meant a lot to me that you liked my writing.

First edition February 2019

ISBN: 978-1-936712-03-8

Published in the United States of America

MURDER, ACTUALLY

To S, with love and gratitude.

CONTENTS

INTRODUCTION

Like brightly colored beads on a string, my life seems to be a succession of vignettes. Characters, conversations, misadventures, and miscalculations by the hundreds. Most of the stories in this book are from my early days as a private detective.

Everything is as true as I remember, though I did change some names and descriptions to protect certain characters.

My life could be divided in two parts: before I became a private detective and after. My career has ascended from stakeout to the rarefied world of the white-shoe, risk-consulting firm, where the cases are more sophisticated, the lawyers' ties more expensive, and the money much better. Stolen-art recovery, money laundering, corporate fraud, intelligence gathering. A lot of that, but I also handle the juicy stuff, as in kidnapping, homicide, rape, and blackmail. I simply love it when everybody is lying right and left.

Becoming a detective changed me or maybe it just allowed me to be *more* of who I always had been. I was the daredevil tomboy and as a detective I found that same breathless, joyful feeling again.

I was named Clarissa after my mother and the three other Clarissas preceding her right back to pre–Civil War Philadelphia. My name as a private detective is Cici, which is much easier when being introduced to a room filled with law enforcement. Cici was never anything but CC, and being called Charlie came about when the men first called me C for Charlie C for Charlie, then Double C, then just plain C or Charlie.

I grew up in Mississippi, escaped the minute I could go away to college, and only went back for visits because Mother still lived there.

I'm five foot nine and weigh 132 pounds, I have shoulder-length dark hair and mud-brown eyes. Once a man compliments my eyes I never take him seriously again.

Divorced with no children, no dependents, unless you count the geraniums on my terrace, my life is fairly unstructured. I do fifty sit-ups every morning, eat Oreos for breakfast, sometimes have popcorn and white wine for dinner. I'm grown up, and I can go to bed whenever I want.

There are no rules because it's too late to die young. Maybe there is reincarnation, maybe not, so I think it is mandatory to lead a life of risk and adventure. This might be your only chance. This minute might be your last chance.

Sail into the eye of the storm. Kiss the risk. As Mario Andretti said, "If things seem under control, you're just not going fast enough."

TAIL

Becoming a private detective meant doing things I had never considered doing, things I had never thought I could do, and being catapulted into situations I had never imagined. I was usually the only female, which made me feel I was being watched closely for signs of weakness, so I gave everything my best, never confessed to being tired, cold, hungry, or deeply confused. I refused to fail in front of an audience that had not deemed me capable in the first place. But the men at Parker's, our illustrious detective agency in Hell's Kitchen, saw that, I think, and were good to me, and, at some point, accepted me as one of them.

One spring day I was sent out to do a U.S. Customs tail in Moby Dick. The whale was a big white van with numerous dings and scrapes and sported a sunroof that was perfect for a periscope. I'd spent days in it eating Chinese food behind blacked-out windows on Canal Street. Usually I rode shotgun, but today I was in the driver's seat on my own, sitting in a parking lot at Kennedy Airport, waiting for the call. The hours wore on. Barefooted, bare legs across the front seat with my khakis pulled up to my knees, getting a bit of a tan. Radioing back and forth with Mas over what to eat, how to find a real lunch, or personal negotiations about whose turn it was to raid the vending machines. Mas was the Indonesian detective at Parker's. Food was peanut butter and crackers, Diet Coke. The usual wildly nutritious lunch.

I called the office on a land line, which meant putting on shoes and walking twenty feet to a phone booth. No news. Two o'clock. Called again. Three o'clock. Nothing. I dared to drive to a customs building at Kennedy and used the ladies' room. Four-fifteen. The cell phone rang. The office told me customs had called. "Green van, Jersey tag, Charlie Whiskey four two seven Frank. Two hundred and forty-five thousand dollars' worth of watches." Generic, of course, and totally legal until the faces are doctored.

Give them fifteen minutes, I thought. *Customs has my cell phone number, and they'll call me.* They did. It rang. "They've cleared customs. Two male Asians."

I got Mas on the radio. "Thirty-three, where are you?"

"I'm one half mile from parking lot facing south."

"Customs just called. They're leaving now. They've cleared customs. Two male Asians. You got the tag?"

"Affirmative."

Finally I saw the van leaving the parking lot. Rear weighted down by all those watches. Moby Dick and me right there. On the tail. New Jersey Turnpike. "Okay, Thirty-three, I can see you. Going south."

As the afternoon wore on, the van was three cars ahead, then four, and then out of sight. I opened the window to clear my head. Inhaled the cold, fresh air like a spaniel. I tried Mas on the radio, but he didn't answer. I was in the far-left lane and could only count the shadows of the cars and think that the fourth one ahead, the big square one, that particular shadow on the shoulder was the green van. I stared, willing it to be so. Third car passed it. Then it passed the fifth car ahead. It was green. The green van. Relief.

Darkness falling like a veil over a picture. The landscape appeared to sink into the mist before me. I could no longer read the plate. The Outerbridge Crossing, great expanse like stepping off the edge of the world. Crossing the river after death in Egypt. The West Bank. Turning on the headlights. Heading south. Mas had fallen away so many miles ago. No radio contact.

Strange feeling of going fast and not having any idea of where. Maybe they were headed to a safe house, maybe somewhere else. Focused entirely on that green van. So dark it was no longer any color. Nothing else in my life mattered. I emptied my mind of everything but those two tail lights. No one expected me home for supper or home to sleep. No one even knew where I was. A chase. The hunt. They wouldn't lose me. I wouldn't let them escape. My two male Asians were chattering away or listening to the radio. They had no idea I existed. Slowed down for the toll. Paid. Grabbed the receipt. They were three lanes over. Pulling out. *Keep them in sight.* That telltale sag in the rear. Oh, those watches are so heavy. Middle lane. Hands on wheel in the ten-four position. Perfect form. Driver's ed in ninth grade. Going seventy-five. Going eighty.

It was now night. Pitch black beyond the soft glow of the highway. Eighty. Eighty-five. Heading south.

Like gulping champagne.

MURDER, ACTUALLY

T he knife flew past my face and went *twack* as it stuck in the wall behind me. I blinked and thought, *God-daaaamn, he's good*. Elbert got up from his desk and walked around me, pulled the knife out of the wall, then sat down again, aimed, and threw it again. *Twack*. It was the hunting knife with the ten-inch blade he usually kept in his boot. The one that caused pandemonium in airports and courthouses.

These talks in Elbert's office were always stimulating. He, like all the detectives I'd worked for, had a flair for the dramatic. Another round trip by Elbert, another sigh as he sank into his chair, and another *twack*. Any closer and I thought I might have to bring up etiquette. What would Amy Vanderbilt say about knife-throwing in office situations? It was the last gasp of 1994, and one would assume we had all evolved.

Elbert was considering sending me to Italy to deal with counterfeiters. I'd heard him out and responded in the affirmative. "Sure. What else do I need to know? Will I be flying into Rome?" I crossed my legs in tight black jeans and noticed my bootlace was untied.

He stroked his short gray beard as I bent down and double-tied a bow. Elbert Parker was somewhere in his fifties but could look anywhere between downright boyish to deeply sleep deprived. This was strange, since his clothes always looked as if he slept in them. He dressed invariably in black, which some of the detectives uncharitably suggested had to with laundry.

His office was a plywood-partitioned, windowless cube at one end of a large room with windows overlooking Twenty-Ninth Street. The agency rented a two-story warehouse between Tenth and Eleventh Avenues; this was Chelsea if you wanted to pretend to be fashionable but was more like a little piece of Hell's Kitchen if you judged it by the populace.

Major hooker territory. I was told that the pimps kept it safe. The girls wore hot pants all year round, and on a day like today shivered in their high-heeled, pastel-colored, patent-leather boots. Their tiny bomber jackets exposed extraordinary breasts. I was very curious about the hookers. I didn't think much of their fashion sense and resented the probability that they were making more money than me but I felt sorry for them, too. I was looking out the window of the second floor one day—in the morning actually—and saw a woman in the front seat of a car moving her head back and forth. I thought, *Wow, somehow she has managed to plug a hair dryer into the cigarette lighter.* One of the ex-cops enlightened me with a big grin. I hated myself for blushing.

Winter on Twenty-Ninth Street was piles of dirty snow. Inside the warehouse we sat at our desks on the ground floor and blew on our hands to keep warm. Mickey brought in a heater and Warner, the boxer, slept in front of its glowing orange teeth all day, but it didn't affect the temperature of the room much.

In summer, Twenty-Ninth Street was odiferous and garbage-strewn. The twenty-four-hour garages were filled with ailing taxi cabs and the eighteen wheelers were loaded with wholesale vegetables. Somebody always had a radio blaring Spanish music. The men were grease-smeared and overalled or T-shirted and jeaned and wearing those wide weightlifter belts.

When I first walked down Twenty-Ninth Street for my interview with Elbert, I smiled and said hello to everybody, and nobody ever treated me like the interloper I felt I was.

Now I stared at Elbert and at the books behind him. *The Oxford Dictionary,* a thesaurus, several atlases, psychology books, woodworking books, books on the CIA, a biography of Jack the Ripper, the complete

Sherlock Holmes. His hat collection was on the top shelf and I could see needed dusting. There were hats for any situation, any occasion: baseball cap and fedora, pith helmet and hardhat.

The vast space beyond Elbert's cubicle had desks, phones, and computers for the two secretaries. A honking horn or a siren from Tenth Avenue added to the basic background noise of ringing phones, the intercom from downstairs, the crackle and then the bark of the two-way radio from Chinatown or Jersey.

My life was punctuated by surveillances, scam calls, and my forays west of Broadway wearing the video camera and lying to everybody. There were days in Chinatown when my eyes would stream with tears because of the cold. On some of these days I was in Moby Dick with Mas, and the idea was to video everybody on Canal Street, on Mott, all over the place. I was wearing the hump, which was Elbert's black vest with the battery pack in the back and the pinhole lens peeking out through a tiny hole in the front. It meant I had to casually leave my parka undone in ten-degree weather, which was just another delightful aspect of the assignment. I'd go out and slowly walk from stall to stall, looking for this or that, asking prices, talking to the vendors for as long as I could stand it. All the while aiming my right breast at face after face, which worked well since I'm five foot nine and the Asians are usually not very tall.

Then I'd walk casually back to the van parked a few blocks away and with one frost-bitten hand pull open the door of Moby Dick and climb up into the front seat. Mas would turn the heat up to full blast, and I'd struggle out of several layers, and then he would retrieve the camera and turn it off while I got warm. In a few minutes, we'd reset it, turn the Power button to On, argue over whether it was going to work or not, then suit me up and I'd go out again.

Elbert was still stroking his beard. He was so lost in thought he'd probably lapsed into alpha waves. I waited for him to answer me about whether I'd be flying in to Rome. He reached for one of his skinny black cigarettes and said, "You'll be flying into Florence as we think the factory is in Tuscany." A wave of excitement swept over me. "I'm waiting for the client to confirm. Your passport in order?"

"Absolutely," I grinned.

"I'll let you know when I hear from Lombardi. He's the lawyer in charge of this. Make sure you're reachable all day."

I left him and sprinted down the stairs to what I called the Southern office, with its nonstop Nashville soundtrack. Delighted about Italy, I kicked open the door thinking I had to find my Italian dictionary.

The legal beagles deemed the Italian caper too risky, so it was canceled. I was sorry, but I wasn't devastated as I had my own drama unfolding in New York.

This story had actually begun one breathlessly hot night on a balcony in Santo Domingo, a year or two earlier, when I still thought of myself as a novelist, when becoming a detective seemed as likely as becoming an astronaut.

Having no apartment in Manhattan led me to live in the oldest hotel in the Western Hemisphere to write a novel. I'd called from New York and spoken with the hotel manager, Fernando, who seemed sweetly Latin and emotional at the prospect of having a writer living at the hotel. Fernando told me there was a writer's rate, quoted me a tiny monthly charge, and asked me to bring him Adidas sneakers, white, size ten.

In Santo Domingo, I swam every morning, dressed, and walked to the main plaza, nodding at the statue of Christopher Columbus, then entered my usual bar and took my usual table, which overlooked the sweating Haitians who were digging up the street in order to lay telephone cables. Without a word exchanged, my waiter would materialize with a ham sandwich and a Diet Coke. I was the only person in the place without a Clark Gable mustache. Dominican men sat at little round tables reading their newspapers in Spanish as I read one section of the Sunday *New York Times*. I rationed myself to one section per day, saving it and savoring it until the new Sunday edition arrived by plane the following Tuesday. The Dominicans and I all read in semi-darkness, under sleepily turning, wooden-bladed ceiling fans as the Haitians outside, stripped to the waist and shining with sweat, swung pickaxes and shouted in Creole.

By eight in the morning I was back at Nicolas de Ovando's house, which had been built in 1498. He was a pal of Christopher Columbus's brother Bartolomeo. De Ovando's portrait hanging in the front hall showed a black-haired, bearded man with the wild eyes of a religious fanatic and/or murderer and, in fact, he had killed thousands of Indians before they were deemed human by a Papal edict. Once, in early-morning gloom, I thought I saw him, complete with sword at his side, in the darkness at the top of the stairs.

My room was high-ceilinged, all white except for dark wooden beams; my small mahogany desk by the window overlooked the Ozama River, littered with big ships heading out to sea. The heat was heavy; the air was still. I wrote, usually wearing only earrings and bikini underpants, with the electric fan trained on me, until the maid came to clean, and then I dressed and walked to the plaza again or read a book in the hallway in one of the big wooden Savonarola chairs. Then I returned and wrote until lunch time, went down and had a swim and a salad, and then wrote again until it was time for dinner, which I usually skipped. I swam again and drank a glass or two of red Chilean wine in the room and read until I felt sleepy. I was a hermit, and it suited me. The novel raced along and was far more real to me than anything that was physically happening. The pages stacked up at a great rate on the little desk under the window sill with the palm fronds reaching toward me like green feathers.

Finally, I had done all I had come to do, and I was departing the capital with only a manuscript. Usually I leave a country with a bit of longing, with promises to come back, with addresses; sometimes I actually feel teary in taxis on the way to the airport. A part of me has mated with a piece of time that has a beginning and an end, and I'm abandoning the territory. But this was different. This was to be a clean getaway.

However, on the next-to-last evening I went out with a painter named Victor whose grandfather had come to the Caribbean from the Canary Islands. We went to a bar called Atlantico, and later we did the merengue, which made me believe that one could conceive on a dance floor. Between dances we talked to friends of his, and a woman said, "You must meet Elizabeth."

The next evening, my last before the early morning flight to New York, I went to meet Elizabeth. She was English, tall, and thin and wore a floor-length black sundress. She was surrounded by Siamese cats, Haitian paintings, and hanging plants. Her house was next door to the home of the Dominican president, who was eighty-eight, blind, and well loved. The night was hot, and Elizabeth and I drank wine and ate cheese, which I knew she had gone to a great deal of trouble to procure, and talked as if we'd known each other for years. It was about two in the morning, a few hours before I was to leave the island, when she gave me Rachel.

"May I tell her you're in New York? May I give her your number?" Elizabeth asked. "She was a journalist in Singapore when I was there with the *Wall Street Journal*, and she's a free spirit like you. You've got a lot in common. She's going through a divorce the way you did. A Canadian divorce. She'll be in Manhattan staying with a friend, and she doesn't really know anybody."

So there was not to be a clear-cut escape from Santo Domingo.

Rachel was laughing. It was a rich, deep laugh that would have turned heads in a restaurant. "So you just kept calling detectives in the Yellow Pages?"

I nodded. "I was working my way through the entire 'Investigators comma Private' section, at a great rate since nobody would see me, and finally I got hired."

We were in my small fourth-floor walk-up apartment, which I called the Crow's Nest. Rachel leaned forward, grinning. She had big, white teeth set in a wide mouth. Her nose was large, her eyes were large, and her dark hair fell below her shoulders. There was so much of big-breasted Rachel. She was an earth-mother sort. Nothing delicate about her. Sometimes I thought she belonged in a painting by Velasquez.

"So what-what-who hired you?" She had a habit of stammering when she was excited. Or when she wasn't. Usually it was the entire word, as if she didn't want the listener to miss it.

"I got hired by the investigator with the worst reputation in New York State. But"—I paused—"he gave me a chance, and I'll always love him for that. So, when I say I worked for Vinny Parco and these men gasp and say things like 'I thought he was in jail,' I just smile and tell them the truth."

"What do you tell them? "

"That he was fabulous to me and that I learned a lot and that nobody else in town would give me a job as a detective." I sipped wine. "So that's how it started."

"Why was he so bad? What was wrong with Vinny Parco?"

I laughed, remembering. "I didn't have the faintest idea why he had such a reputation, so when I finally had the interview with him I was floored. He was this charming, self-deprecating Italian who looked as if he should be drinking wine at some little trattoria in Naples. He was *so* Italian and you know how much I love Italy."

"How long did you live in Rome?"

"I guess it was at least five, maybe six years? Two different stints. It flew." I sighed. "Anyway, here was this rather short, stocky man with a shaved head and a walrus mustache and this twinkle in his eye and I liked him. He used to come bombing into the office complaining about how long it took him to shave his head. And I knew when I saw little pinches of bloody toilet paper on his scalp not to ask him anything until after lunch. Beginning of a bad day."

I stopped. Such a long story and it felt like such a long time ago but it wasn't. "Anyway, to answer your question. Vinny got involved with a client who said she thought her husband was having an affair and might kill her, might get her out of the way. She hired Vinny to watch her husband, and he shouldn't have done it, but he gave the client a gun for protection." I rolled my eyes. "And not only that but he gave her a silencer." I grimaced. "Did you know that it's illegal to even own a silencer, let alone use one, let alone for a detective to give one plus a gun to a client?" I didn't wait for Rachel to answer. "By the way, you can use a potato. You don't even *need* a silencer." I sighed in exasperation as Rachel laughed. "It's just the apex of stupid. She told Vinny she needed the silencer so she could practice shooting in the woods in Westchester County and not have the neighbors hear! And he believed her! Well, she was beautiful, and Vinny, of course and as usual, wanted to get her into bed. Anyway, the client, Carolyn Warmus, killed the wife of her lover—yes, she really suckered Vinny in, and it went to trial, and Vinny was the only connection to the gun, and all hell broke loose." I sipped wine. "He was on the stand day after day telling the world what a mistake he'd made."

I thought of Vinny, in a frozen shrug with fingers outspread, that day we were alone in his office. *"Ask me anything. I'll tell ya the truth. Just ask me. I made a big mistake and I paid for it."* Shaking his head, contrite as a small boy who'd broken a window with a baseball, utterly miserable as he remembered.

Rachel leaned forward. "So this was your first boss? Did he tell you all this or did somebody else? "

"I had the interview with him and went right to the library on Fifth and checked out the microfiche for all the news of the trial."

"So being-being a journalist—does it really help when you're a detective?"

"Oh, sure it does. You would have done the same thing. You could do what I do. Maybe you'd do it better."

"I doubt it. Running around Chinatown in vans. Sitting up all night in parked cars . . ."

"You could do it," I said. "I'm not saying you're deranged enough to want to."

Rachel laughed her big laugh. "I am so happy Elizabeth told me to call you. I just . . . New York is . . . is . . . I don't know what it is. But you—living in Rome and Geneva and London and Cyprus and coming back here and starting over, it's just... I feel you've lived my life! And we both had marriages in Canada."

"And neither marriage worked," I said.

She nodded. "And I don't know but"—she flipped her long hair over her shoulders—"I don't-don't have many friends here."

"But didn't you say you were living with a friend in the Village? "

She grabbed her wine glass and took a swallow. "Yes, well, it's Soho. But it's complicated." I waited. "He—Bob is—I met him about ten years ago at a big party in New York. It was before-before I married Ted."

Ted was American; he'd moved to Canada to take a job with an oil company. An engineer. He was a good engineer, but as a husband he didn't work out. Rachel was now in the process of divorcing him.

"And was it love at first sight?"

"No! We slept together a few times all those years ago, but it became a friendship thing. It didn't-didn't go anywhere really. He's a great person, and I like him a lot, but I guess the chemistry was-was bad." I didn't comment and suddenly she smiled sheepishly. "You know what it was? He was terrible in bed." I winced. "He just wasn't... well, he—"

"I get it. You don't have to give me details." I poured wine into both our glasses. Women who say too much make me cringe. I get embarrassed hearing it, not only for myself but also for the absent male.

She began again. "So anyway, we were friends, and then I married Ted. We stayed friends—I'd introduced him to Ted—and when-when I'd come down from Montreal I'd stay with him. Ted thought this was fine; he didn't mind. Actually, Ted and I both-both stayed with him a few times. And Bob has this huge place. A loft. We've been friends for a-a long time."

I sensed there was a lot more to this.

Rachel took a sip of wine and swallowed. "Last spring I came to New York, and I told him that I was getting a divorce, and we drank wine, and he was-was very sweet about the whole thing. He told me if I ever needed a place to stay to-to call him. Then when I left Ted last June I went to New

Hampshire. I have this house up-up there I bought with money my mother left me. So I was in the woods up there all-all summer just getting my thoughts together, and finally just before Thanksgiving I-I decided that I should come to New York and meet people and see if I could get a career going. Bob said-said great, and I've been here two months now."

Snow was falling out the window of my apartment. I imagined I could hear it landing like feathers on the skylights, but, of course, I couldn't. The pâté was gone. The brie was a glorious, gooey mess. The blue candles were burnt down to an inch, and the wax dripped over the Portuguese candlesticks and onto the carved Mexican chest that was my coffee table. The bottle of red wine was nearly empty. This was the moment a guest usually told me everything.

"Any chance you'll be attracted to him again? I mean, you once were."

"No. We just-just get along so well."

She raised her broad shoulders in the baggy black sweater then let them drop like a little girl called on in class. "It's so complicated! I really wish I knew. I wish I could." She poured the last of the wine into her glass and greedily gulped. "Do you have another bottle?"

I got up and took four steps to the kitchen but stayed in the living room to open the half fridge. It was that sort of kitchen and that sort of apartment. You had to be an Olympic gymnast to reach food because you couldn't open the fridge if you were actually in the kitchen and even if you stood in the living room it would only open about eight inches. It reminded me of parking too close to another car. "White okay?"

"Sure. I hope-hope you don't think I have a drinking problem."

"Never. But after we kill this we're going to an AA meeting."

Rachel gave a short laugh, but then became solemn. "Actually Bob came to see me-me in New Hampshire last summer and I told him one of the disappointments in my marriage was—say, do you have any kids?" I shook my head, and she followed up with, "Did you want them? Do you want them?"

"You can't do everything. I've done other things. The timing is never right. To get it all in order at once takes more than luck—the right man as the right father, a roof over your head." What I wasn't saying was that I felt conservative enough to want the child to be born of two strongly connected people and I never seemed to want to be strongly connected. "If a child suddenly appeared at my door I know I would be good to it. I would be kind. Even tender. I would teach it about right and wrong. I would be—"

Rachel was struggling with the corkscrew as I meandered. "But . . ."—I sighed—"I don't know really. The idea of living in one place—one town—long enough for them to get through school, and buying all those shoes. The perpetually growing feet, you know. And making enough peanut butter sandwiches to stretch out a kitchen window to the moon and back. No. Maybe I don't want children."

We both laughed as the cork popped out. I suddenly thought of birth control and laughed again. Let others go forth and multiply. Just let me fornicate happily.

Rachel, full of her own thoughts, splashed wine into the goblets. God, I was going to feel rotten at five a.m. I reached for the glass anyway.

"Well, I wanted-wanted them and Ted didn't. We talked; we discussed; we fought. I considered tricking him, having an accident, and praying he'd be happy after the fact, but-but I think he knew me too well." She flipped her hair over her shoulders, then reached up with both hands and twisted it into a knot. She was silent, then let the curtain of dark hair fall and reached for her wine. "Bob wants a child. And so do I. I'm thirty-eight, and it's something I want. The ex-experience of it. I'm afraid to let too much time go by. You know how you're-you're constantly reading about the fertility rate dropping for women every-every single minute after they turn twenty-two?" She took a swallow of wine, then put down the glass and looked directly at me with her big dark eyes. "I might as well tell you." She paused. "Bob and I are-are going to have a child together."

I got off my second bus at seven-fifteen and slogged knee-deep in snow over to the curb and onto the sidewalk. I waved at Angelo hurrying along bearing a cardboard tray of coffees and teas and bagels. We'd call Poppy's for this and that all day, which meant Angelo got plenty of exercise.

Twenty-Ninth Street was eerily silent. It was bitter cold. The trucks weren't on the street and the hookers weren't hooking. I walked as quickly as I could over the ice, reached the warehouse and kicked the door open. The air was gray with smoke.

Mickey was leaning back in his chair at his desk directly in front of me. "Hey, Charlie. What's up?"

Years ago, Mickey's career as a cameraman at NBC had been disrupted by a strike, so he'd turned to being a P.I. in the interim; the strike ended, but he never went back. He had a high school education, I think, and had, at one point, trained to be an electrician. The lack of formal education didn't matter to me because he was bright and intuitive and *got* people. He understood body language and appreciated nuance. Law school, Harvard, whatever—often the higher education of other men I knew did no good at all in the situations that I thought really counted. My ex-husband, for instance, had degrees from places like the London School of Economics, but he didn't *get* people.

Mickey had a boyish cowlick and eyes that could look greenish with the right shirt. Born in Greenwich Village and still lived there, but he would scoff and correct me by saying it was the Lower East Side. When he was about eleven he parked cars for Vinny the Chin Gigante who now roamed the streets in a bathrobe feigning insanity to fend off indictments for just about everything. Mickey would probably be mobbed up by now, a made man, if he'd been Italian instead of Irish.

Mickey was the youngest at Parker's but he basically ran the show. One afternoon I told him he was the alpha male and that all the men knew it.

"Hey, C." This came from Bobby, sipping tea out of a Styrofoam cup. He was well over six foot four in the cowboy boots he lived in. His Stetson with a turkey feather made him even taller. Bobby was going bald but let his dark blond hair grow past his shoulders, he had very few teeth behind a full moustache, and his massive arms were covered with tattoos of naked women. Very intimidating until I noticed his kind blue eyes and saw how gentle he was. This tough guy played the bagpipes, dried flowers and made jam. An ex-cop from Pennsylvania who drove into the office at two a.m. on Mondays and spent the weeknights in a sleeping bag with the dog, watching a TV with a five-inch screen. He was always available for any kind of night duty whether it was a tail, dumpster diving, or a garbage grab. Then on Fridays he drove back home to his wife.

"Hey, C, did you run the DMV on that guy from yesterday?" Vinny was at the far desk. I know my stories have too many Vinnys but every P.I. firm in New York has a Vinny. At least one.

"I ran it but I didn't get it. We owe them money." I dropped my bag on my desk, plopped on my chair and started to pull off the soaked boots. The air was thick with "What the fuck is going on!" and the answer, "The same old fucking thing!"

The men would pay for gas and rent cars on their own credit cards hoping that Parker's wouldn't go bankrupt before they were reimbursed. Milli, the Puerto Rican secretary, guarded the checkbook and wielded the power that went with it like a marine. She was beautiful until you knew her. She had black shining hair and bright eyes and an even white smile, but once you heard her chew someone to pieces over not putting a file back, you re-assessed her attractiveness. Milli possessed a machete of a tongue.

I sighed as I pulled off wet socks and then searched my desk drawer for a clean pair,

There were benefits to having an office in a warehouse. The place was jammed with baseball caps, T-shirts, jeans, purses, watches, neckties, leather jackets, key chains, toys, even socks. All emblazoned with the logos of cartoon stars and sports teams and French and Italian family names like Chanel and Fendi.

Vinny was already on the phone to upstairs. He was shouting than banged down the receiver and sucked on his cigarette. "She says our account is in the negative for three fucking dollars and twelve fucking cents. What the fuck does that mean?" There was a chorus of complaints and actual roars from the men.

Vinny lived on Staten Island, which was exotic to me since I'd never been there. Zanzibar, the Aeolian Islands, all sorts of islands but not to Staten Island. Vinny was blond and blue-eyed with a handsome, open face. Married, with four kids and way-up-there blood pressure which might have been why he had such rosy cheeks.

The door slammed and Mas walked in. He was Indonesian, five foot three and weighed about a hundred and ten pounds. "So what's up?" he asked and was greeted with the complaints about Milli and the precarious financial situation.

He shrugged then fell to his knees to pet Warner.

"Hi, guys." The door slammed and Elbert materialized. A vision in black from square-toed Frye boots to black felt, wide-brimmed hat. Warner bobbed up and down in a state of ecstasy, her little nub of a tail wagging.

"Why don't we follow up on that new Canal Street location and get somebody down there before they open at ten?" Elbert was saying.

Mickey was writing. "I'll get Mas to go. Is Sharif coming in today?"

"He was here yesterday," said Mas. He was putting film in a camera. No one responded to this revelation. Mas possessed a logic that often defied us and sometimes made us scream in frustration. On the other hand, this logic was the logic of our prey.

After a moment of silence, Elbert spoke. "So we don't know if Sharif is coming in, is that it?" He sighed and lit a cigarette, then snapped the lighter closed.

Sharif often called me on the phone late at night and told me he didn't want to work for Parker's. All he wanted was to be an accountant. The tall, thin, elegantly handsome Mauritanian was worried about getting killed in Chinatown. The spying, the lying, the wearing a wire, the betrayal of the bad guys we persuaded to trust us and made deals with—yes, okay, it was risky. Reliable in his own original way, he only worked when his horoscope told him it was auspicious.

"Okay, Charlie, you want to go with Mas and sit on One Twenty-Four and do a couple of fly-bys at these other locations?" Mickey tore off a notebook sheet with addresses.

I took the page, stuffed it into my jeans pocket, and started pulling on my spare boots. I knew the drill by now. Tags, faces, watching. Estimating how much product was in the shop, who was there, who came, possible relationship. Any delivery. How much. Back exits. Storage areas. The occasional leap from the van to follow someone through the crowded streets. Looking for lookouts or spotters.

Mas tossed me a radio and I turned it on and off and on and listened then dropped it into my canvas bag along with a notepad, pens, a black beret, a fistful of toilet paper, and a rubber band. I was prepared. It would be a good day except for the cold.

Mas and I, dressed for the Arctic, slammed the door then started across the slush of Twenty-Ninth Street to Mustafa's garage. In minutes we were in Moby Dick, racing down the West Side Highway toward Chinatown.

"What have you been up to?" Rachel's deep voice came from my answering machine. "Call me and let's get together."

I deleted the message and sat down in one of my Chinese Chippendale chairs. What had I been up to? Exhausted, I broke my own rule and snapped open a Diet Coke at seven o'clock. Swigging at the bubbles, I knew I could drug myself with Benadryl if the caffeine bothered me at eleven. I would also slip into a bubble bath to relax my muscles before bed. Bubbles kept me alive.

I hesitated to call her back. Baron von Alvensleben was in town this week from Geneva, and I was to meet him somewhere for dinner or Saturday brunch, there was a concert and dinner with Larry and an art gallery opening. It almost seemed like too much to do anything but that, other than work, in the span of a week. How absurd to be so tired. What a relief not to be in love.

I picked up the phone and punched in the loft's number.

Rachel and I met at a little restaurant on Lexington in the Fifties and ordered pasta and salads. She was working on a screenplay, and we talked about plot, and she was reading one of my books, so we talked about that. As always, she swished her hair back and forth like a pony and nervously twisted one long dark strand around her forefinger as she leaned toward me. "I don't have-have anyone to really talk to," she said as we were paying the bill.

I was taken aback. "What about Bob? "

We stood up and she shook her head. "No. I mean I can talk to him about everything except what I really *need* to talk about."

She pulled on her coat and we headed for the door. Once out on the sidewalk she said, "Do you—do you want have another drink somewhere?" I knew she meant my apartment so I suggested it and soon we were up the three flights of stairs sitting in front of a bottle of wine.

"I'm having problems getting pregnant." She screwed up her face. "I think Bob has the problem, but how do we know? I'll be thirty-nine in six months! Anyway, yesterday we had some tests at this clinic and . . ."

"Rachel, sometimes it takes awhile. All you have to do is pick up any magazine and see that the country is full of women trying to get pregnant." I paused. "And I've spent my whole life trying *not* to."

She laughed then. "God, I know. Isn't it ridiculous? You think it'll happen by accident all those times when you're fooling around in college, and you panic when it's a day late and-and here I am counting days and counting off weeks and"—she gave a growl of frustration—"and it's a little artificial maybe. Yes, maybe that's it."

"What do you mean?" I poured the wine and stuck the cork back into the bottle. I wasn't the least bit tired but thought it would be five o'clock and my alarm would be going off in no time if we talked the way we had the other evenings.

"Well, Bob and I are-are friends and we don't want to get married and we don't want to fall in love."

"You don't?" I interjected, suddenly feeling outrageously conservative and even slightly romantic.

"No. We wanted it to be clear from the beginning. Very precise. We have very strict guidelines about this whole thing."

"But you're having this baby together so you have to—"

"Well, of course, we have to. That's sort of the odd thing about this because I don't really-really like it with him and I don't think he cares one way or the other, but we don't-don't want it to interfere with the day-to-day stuff." She took a swallow of wine. "I mean I like Bobby a lot. Really a lot. I've known him ten years and he's a good friend but the sex is not-not good. "

I waited then said, "So I guess you're sort of careful about the day of the month and that's it."

"Well, more than that. We decided it wouldn't be right to do it in-in the apartment because then we'd be reminded of it, so, on my most fertile day, we check into a hotel."

I laughed. I couldn't help it. The laugh leapt out of me.

"I'll tell-tell you how it works. We go out to dinner and we go to-to the theater and then we go to a big suite in the Plaza and once it was the Pierre and we-we turn on the TV and we do it."

"That bad, huh?"

She nodded and wrinkled her nose. "That's what I mean about artificial."

"So you really aren't attracted to him? Don't want to marry him? But you do want to be parents? Together?"

She nodded vehemently. "We have-have it all worked out. I will be the primary caregiver and will have the child with me. He will have unlimited visiting privileges. He will-will pay for everything, but I will decide where the child goes to school. Holidays we'll decide as they come up, but day to day the-the child will live with me. Whether it's in Hong Kong or on a ranch in Wyoming."

Rachel was counting her every cent, she'd told me, and every time I saw her she was wearing the same black outfit. It was a shift for me to think of her as having money, to imagine her suddenly belonging anywhere but Soho. But that was silly of me. She belonged anywhere she wanted. She was a freelance journalist, a wanderer with an unhappy childhood from some small town in Ohio—the whole point of Rachel was to fit in anywhere she chose. Her black clothes, the wild hair, the heavy, thick-soled boots with a tread like a tractor's were the uniform of any bohemian writer in Paris or London. She'd fit in. And with money, she could decide at what level, garret or penthouse.

"What if you marry someone and have a second child?"

"That's fine-fine with him. We've talked about it."

"What if he marries someone and she can't have children and she wants to raise his child and puts pressure on him to obtain custody?"

"No. That won't happen."

I could tell she hadn't thought of it, and that scared me. "What if he doesn't like your husband who will be the father figure on the scene?"

"He trusts me—trusts me enough to make a good choice." She looked up at me with those big, long-lashed dark eyes.

"Do you think he will be a good father?"

She nodded. "Yes, I-I really do. He is kind, he is very intelligent, and he wants—he wants this baby as much—as much as I do." She paused. "Bobby's had a tough time. His mother died when he was about six or seven. She fell and he saw the whole thing and he isn't—he isn't close to his brothers or his sister. He's-been-been alone for most of his life."

"But you don't want to be with him, to live together with the baby?"

"That won't happen. We-we don't want it to. That's why we—"

"You're sure you don't want it?"

"I'm sure. He'll be able to visit me-me and the baby whenever he wants, to stay with us, to be nearby. We are intelligent, realistic. It'll be shared-shared custody."

"Are you going to work after the baby comes? Do you think you'll want to?"

"I could. Of course, I can write anywhere."

"But will Bob suddenly say, as some divorced parents do, I don't want you to move across the country with *my* child? What if somebody wants you to ghost-write a book in Russia?"

She didn't answer right away. She seemed to be considering whether to tell me something or not. "Bob has money." She took a sip of wine. "His-his family is in real estate. They own a lot of real estate. They don't come out and flaunt it like Donald Trump, but the money is there."

"So the child—and you—will be taken care of."

She nodded. "It doesn't matter where I want to live. Bob could always get to me to-to see the baby. He might-might come, or he might send tickets. The money-money doesn't matter."

An hour later we hugged goodnight and I heard her clump down the stairs and wondered if we'd woken up Marvin, whose apartment was just across the hall. I brushed my teeth and crawled into the sleeping bag. I lay down and thought, cripes, four hours till I pull on boots and head across town to Twenty-Ninth Street. Four hours to close my eyes and not think. The words floated through my mind. The money doesn't matter. I thought, no, it doesn't. It's the baby. Then I thought, no. The only thing that matters is sleep.

It was a cold winter. I spent lots of days in Chinatown watching doorways and making buys in one stall after another, noting who was there, nationality, height, weight, distinguishing features, how much product, any doors, storage rooms. Everything I could notice and absorb went into my reports typed back at the office. Sometimes I drew floor plans and these were faxed to law enforcement.

Rachel called when she needed to see me. We never had the long phone conversations I had with other friends, leaving me with an aching ear and an urgent need for a glass of water. For talking she really liked coming to my apartment and indulging in marathon wine drinking.

"It's like Europe," she said. "I always think I'm in Rome or Paris when I come up those stairs and then to be here with all your paintings and the candles. It's a great apartment."

"Thanks. I love the Crow's Nest. It's microscopic, but the location's good. It's the cheapest I could find when I was just starting to be a detective. I was scared to death I wouldn't be able to pay the rent."

I would never say that to some of my friends, but I knew Rachel would understand. The year before, working for Vinny Parco, I remembered one woman who, upon discovering that I was paid ten dollars an hour as a detective, screamed and said, "But I give my cleaning woman twelve!"

I shrugged and said, "Well, I started at eight." Her investment banker husband took me aside after dinner and said, very quietly, "You know you could apply for food stamps." I smiled sweetly and sipped the hundred-year-old brandy.

I harbored no jealousy toward any cleaning woman, and I could still afford occasional forays to the grocery store so the comment was simply air. I thought of myself as in the bracket with the artists and wannabe actors I knew. I was with those forty million Americans who couldn't afford health insurance. My "entertaining" was wine from Garnet's up the street and cheese, pâté, and baseball bats of baguettes from the Egyptian's on First. Always better than being coerced into going out and splitting a dinner tab with a woman, which I could not do. And the talking was always easier than in a noisy restaurant. There were men in my life, but no one who fascinated me at the moment. Dinners and conversation. No physical stuff. No one I was in love with.

Maybe there was another factor. The men in the office occasionally joked about it. They only knew because one morning I got my nightgown jammed in the zipper of my sleeping bag. Trapped, I wriggled like a worm across the room wondering what I'd tell 9-1-1 if I couldn't jockey into position to reach the scissors in my desk drawer. Anyway, as Elbert announced to all in the Southern office, "Don't ever again ask her why she was late for work. C, we can't take the truth." He was laughing. "Don't tell us."

"So you don't sleep in a bed?" Rachel was saying.

"Thought it would take up too much room. With all the bookcases lining the walls where would I put it?"

"Your books are really more important, aren't they?"

"Yes! And I sleep really well. I imagine I'm an Indian in the woods or a sailor on the deck of a ship. I can sleep under the window and actually see the moon between those two big buildings on Third."

She poured me more wine. "I think falling asleep under the moon in Manhattan is pretty great."

"I'm glad you appreciate it. There are those who do not," I said. "To change the subject—I have so many things I want to talk about, that I want to ask you—I know you were in Singapore and Hong Kong for years, but I want to know what sort of articles you wrote. So many things I want to know! Tell me the best thing you did in Asia."

"Hmmmm." She rolled her eyes upward. "I interviewed the King of Afghanistan for a magazine in London and they liked it. They published it. I was very proud of myself."

"That's really great! I never met him, but I knew his son in Rome. Prince Alexander. Did you meet him?" She shook her head. "He was big, tall, and handsome and wore cowboy boots." I remembered coming home in the evening and finding notes from him on my bureau. He would get the cleaning woman to let him in to my apartment. It had bothered me. "All these Afghans—the king and his retinue—lived outside Rome in a sort of compound. The king played backgammon all night long." Rachel giggled huskily. "Years before, when I arrived in Afghanistan they wouldn't let us get off the plane right away because they were laying down the red carpet for the king who had just arrived on another plane. That was the last year of his reign. The next year his brother took over the country in that bloodless coup d'état while the king was off in Italy seeing doctors." I sighed. "So I saw him but not up close, and you actually got to talk to him!"

"Yeah, but you-you knock me out," Rachel said with a trace of awe in her voice. "You've lived my life! We've done all the same things! All this traveling, all this independence. It takes a certain kind of person to love it or-or to even do it or maybe I should say, to survive it! What we have doesn't work in Canada." She shook her head. "Just doesn't! Elizabeth told me I-I would like you. I'm so glad she gave me your name. I need someone to talk to. I've tried to see a few of my old-old friends here and it's not the same."

"It never is. Been to your high school reunion lately?" I winced.

Rachel laughed. One of her big snort ones. "A nightmare come true. Best-best thing is the revenge of the geeks. The metamorphosis of the losers." She then became serious. "But you would think, I mean, I would think that women you met in your adult life would be—well, anyway, they are *not*. We don't really click anymore. One-one woman friend—did I tell you about Stacy?" I shook my head. "She was the one, all those years ago, who took me to the party where-where I met Bob. I thought she, of all people, would understand. But I told-told her about the baby and how we would bring him or her up and she was—I don't know. Let's say very put off by the situation. Then she started-started talking to me about right and wrong and I left the restaurant."

I blurted out exactly what I was thinking. "Did she think you were having a baby for money?"

"Guess that was it." Rachel rolled her eyes.

"Has he ever wanted a child before now? Didn't you say he was in his fifties?"

"He says he wanted one when he was-was married but it didn't work out. She was in med school and the marriage ended."

"How long has he been divorced?"

"Well, he's not-not really divorced." Rachel twirled one long lock of dark hair around her finger.

"Separated?"

"Ummm, well, I mean, she-she disappeared." Taking a deep breath, she plunged on. "They weren't getting along and they were going to get a divorce, except Bobby didn't want a divorce and she-she disappeared. It was in all the papers."

"Disappeared? I don't get it. What do you mean exactly?"

"She left the apartment one morning, and he never-never saw her again." Her voice was light, her manner nonchalant.

"Did she run away? Start a new life somewhere?"

"They don't think so, but they don't know. Nobody knows what happened to her. She just disappeared."

"That's crazy. That's horrible. Did he tell you that?"

"I had read about it but didn't connect it with him when I met him at the party ten years ago. He told me—told me when we were having the love affair, that his wife had disappeared. He didn't think he'd ever see her again."

"What do you think about it?"

She pulled at a strand of dark hair. "I feel sorry for him. What a terrible thing to have to go through."

"Were they separated when it happened?"

"No. But I think they were spending weekends-weekends apart or maybe just weekends together. I don't know. Anyway, he wanted to save-save the marriage and she wanted out and one day she left the apartment and he never saw her again." She took a sip of wine.

"Did he try to find her?"

"Oh, yes. He did everything you could imagine. He hired private detectives to-to check all the mental hospitals and the morgues, and he went and saw-saw everybody with a head injury or amnesia in her age range. His father hired people to look for her, too."

I didn't say anything. My mind was racing. Real estate. Money. Missing wife.

"He really tried. He really tried to find her."

Rachel left at midnight in a flurry of black, swinging the big cape around herself and clunking down the stairs in her thick-soled, industrial-strength boots. I was tired but couldn't sleep. I kept thinking of someone disappearing. In New York. Leaving a building, out on a sidewalk, never being seen again.

"Hey, what's going on? Hot date?" This interrogation greeted me when I slammed the door one Thursday morning.

I could tell they approved of my wool slacks and the sweater and blazer, and it both pleased and embarrassed me. In the beginning I'd wanted to be as much like the men as I could and had headed straight for the Gap to try on eleven styles of jeans until I had the perfect ones. I bought three pairs of jeans and then three pairs of khakis and that was it. The wardrobe. The slightest deviation from the uniform was invariably commented upon.

Today there was the murmuring and then, "So who is he, C?" and I said it was a she, just a friend. The talk swerved to Canal Street, to personalities, and invariably, to money and, more specifically, the lack of it. The day was a blur of ringing phones, a couple of scam calls, and one walk over to a Broadway location where I used fake business cards and pretended to be named Veronica, pretended to want to buy wholesale for my boutique. The boutique I'd invented and named on the way up in the stinking-with-urine elevator.

Finally, at six, when I'd turned off my computer, gathered my bag, put on lipstick and was ready to leave, I couldn't stand it so I said, "Hey, has anybody here ever heard about the Durst disappearance? That young wife who just vanished about twelve years ago?"

Elbert puffed on his cigarette. "I remember something about it. Everyone thought the husband had masterminded it, but nothing could be proved. Papers had a field day."

"Did he do it?" I asked.

"I'd say he did it. He was the only one with anything to gain. Robert Durst was his name." Elbert blew smoke out of his nose.

Mickey looked up from his computer. "Why do you care, Charlie?"

"Because I'm having dinner with him tonight."

Mas gave me a ride down to Greene Street in a driving rainstorm. Thunder crashed around us and lightning split the sky above the Hudson. It was a strange storm. A warm spell on a winter day and now this. "Why you meeting this guy. What for?" asked Mas.

"He's a friend of a friend of mine. She wants me to. And I'm curious."

Mas changed lanes with a vengeance, and horns blared in a cacophony of rage over the roar of the rain. The little Indonesian who could barely see over the steering wheel never bothered to glance in the rearview mirror. "Fuck them," he said with quiet dignity. He turned to me. "You always curious. You more curious than anybody. Except Mickey. Mickey is most curious of anyone."

"I want to know what's going on, Mas. Why, why, why, why. You know I used to be a journalist."

"Yeah, me, too."

"I thought you were a freedom fighter and then a driver for those ambassadors to the UN. Like Boutros Boutros Ghali."

"Yeah, all that. Boutros Boutros. Nice guy. And I was journalist, too. But why you want to have dinner with somebody who make his wife disappear? Maybe he make you disappear, too."

I laughed, thinking of the comments as I'd left the office. Basically, it was the consensus of opinion that I was a piece of work but, even so, they were primed to come after me if I didn't show up tomorrow. My personal knights. My avenging angels in jeans. "Maybe, Mas, but I'm ready."

"You not armed," he scoffed.

"I have my Swiss army knife," I said as I opened the door and prepared to leap across rushing gutter water as wide as a creek. "You never know when you'll need a corkscrew."

I was unprepared for the loft. The elevator, rather industrial and spartan, had given no indication of the luxury awaiting me upstairs. Rachel threw her arms around me and loudly announced my arrival, and I slipped out of a dripping raincoat. She led me into about three thousand feet of polished wooden floor lit by track lights high above our heads; it was starkly modern. The rain drummed on the roof and beat on the skylights.

"Where's Bob?" I asked as she led me toward a very large kitchen of blond wood, chrome, and glass. A dining room table was set with woven mats of pale straw and candles in hurricane globes.

"He's probably still playing with his computer. He does a lot of work from home nowadays. Hardly goes into the office at all." She gestured vaguely toward a faraway desk and I could see a lamp, a wing chair and a figure bent over a laptop. "Help me finish the salad."

The kitchen had the newest implements on the market and I was reminded of a movie set. So very Williams Sonoma. Rachel washed and dried lettuce as I made the dressing, something I did learn during my marriage to a gourmet. Then I went back and forth to the table with the salt and pepper and the salad forks.

"So what do you think? Do you think you can learn anything from a writing class or should I just forget it?" Rachel wrinkled her forehead. "Or should I just use it for structure and write the screenplay my own way? Do you think it would help me?"

"I don't know. I don't think a writing class can make someone who can't write into someone who can write. You are obviously a writer so you're way ahead. I think that it can make a writer a better writer. It could probably give you new ways to approach what you want to write about."

Rachel took napkins out of a lacquered wicker basket and folded them. "So you think I should do it?"

"Why not? If you have the time and the money, do it." I grabbed the napkins and added them to the three place settings.

"I've heard everything about you." The voice was behind me; I turned to see a smallish, slender man no taller than five foot six.

"And you still want to have dinner with me?" I smiled.

He didn't smile back but moved toward the kitchen.

Rachel made small talk about the salad, the pasta. She was on the other side of the butcher block. A figure in black, as usual. Tights and baggy long sweater and black, clunky boots. Robert sort of moused around. He lit the first candle at the far end of the table. He was bespectacled, with colorless eyes; his dark hair was going gray.

"So you're in New York again," he said. "Traveled all over the world and you are finally back." He bent over the table concentrating on one flickering candle and I stared at the nondescript face illuminated by the flame.

"New York's my favorite place these days," I said.

He had small ears and a thin-lipped mouth. There was nothing sensuous about him, I decided, but his intelligence could make him attractive. He had nice hands. Not particularly small hands, as one would expect from looking at his small frame. Rachel had told me he was fiftyish and he looked it.

Conversation at dinner was pleasant enough. I asked him about the loft. "Put my townhouse on the market last year. Just thought I wanted to live down here for a change. That same day somebody at the firm called about this place, and I saw it at lunchtime and signed all the papers before the banks closed. Done." This was delivered without the hint of a smile.

"Wow," I marveled. "It's a fantastic space!"

Rachel got up to get the pepper grinder and then stood behind him mouthing the words *Do you like him? Do you like him?* She could have been in the fourth grade. I stifled a smile.

We talked about where we'd been, not in one of those one-upmanship games, but more in the vein of "I was impressed by" or "I felt . . ." I said that my biggest surprise was to finally see the Taj Mahal and to think that it surpassed the splendor of every photograph. Robert said he'd felt that way about the Matterhorn. He actually used the word *surprised*. I was surprised that anything did. He was a pale, soft-spoken person with a sense of entitlement. His clothes were typically yuppie, falling somewhere between the Gap and Ralph Lauren, but the aura was one of "I can afford the best but it doesn't matter. This is what I've chosen to put on." Khakis, topsiders, and crew-neck sweater of moss green. I had the feeling he had not been out in the driving rain or even out of the apartment that day or maybe not even for the past several days.

Bob disliked Switzerland, and I found myself trying not to sound defensive. "I was surprised by Geneva," I said, assuming he would ask why. He didn't. That was his way. He would withdraw. With some people you might think it was because they didn't want to show their ignorance or because they weren't interested, but with Robert—he had stopped being Bob to me—I wondered if it was because he didn't want to imply that your idea was important to him. You weren't allowed to dispute what he'd just said. He got the last word not by following your last word but rather by letting yours hang there, unacknowledged. It was a very real power he possessed.

And yet, he was so physically unprepossessing. There was not any hint of an athlete about him. You might call him wiry but you could also describe him as frail. I could see this was a man who not only got what he wanted but expected to get what he wanted. Rachel, on the other hand, was warm and giving and interjected only to emphasize how much she agreed with him. The play between them fascinated me. Now docile, she was unlike the woman I knew when she was in my apartment. Her posture, her entire demeanor was changed.

We all had strong opinions about California. He'd graduated from Berkeley with an MBA in the early 1970s. "Can't imagine you as a hippie," Rachel said. She giggled in that husky way of hers.

"I marched," he said cryptically as he speared a sprig of watercress. "But I didn't wear love beads or flowers in my hair. I didn't go *that* far."

"Well, you were a business major, after all," I interjected. "Part of the military industrial complex."

He wasn't amused. I hadn't meant to be anything but light; I'd meant to elicit a smile.

I tried not to watch him. Part of me wanted to scream "What did you do with her? How did you get away with it?" Robert Durst with his soft voice, I decided, was pathologically controlling. I bet that the softer his voice became the more aggressive he became. I imagined the dining room table as a board room table. He was used to wielding power. He was also very comfortable having Rachel get up, bring dishes to him, serve him first, and clear it all away afterward. My attempts to help her were waved aside. By him. He was used to servants. Rachel fell into that role like a 1950s housewife. The subservience of this big, gawky, outspoken woman astonished me. I knew her well enough to realize that she'd turned down the volume of her laugh. That was a good thing, but she'd turned down the force of her opinions, too.

Yes, I know it was partly her natural warmth, her very nature that made sure he had enough wine in his glass or that he had more parmesan, but it would have taken so much effort for me to summon those qualities in the face of Robert. He was definitely a Robert to me and not a soft Bob or Bobby. That first dinner I saw him as cool, even cold. Rachel was the light in his darkness. She was benevolent and even maternal.

And I was? I don't know what I was. I suppose I was the watcher.

"So what was he like?" asked Mickey. We were alone in the office the following afternoon. It was pouring rain outside.

"He's small, reminded me of Woody Allen. But he doesn't have that nervous, outward, twitchy show of insecurity. Whatever tension there is, it's coiled inside." I turned back to my computer and to the report on the T-shirt factory in Queens. "Probably been going to a shrink since the third grade."

"Think he did it?"

"Did what?"

"Made his wife disappear."

I shrugged and kept typing.

Mickey said, "Let's call it murder. It is murder, actually." Then he asked, "What do you have to do with this, Charlie? Can't you find anybody better to have dinner with?"

I made a face and looked over at him. "I met this friend of a friend. This all started in Santo Domingo. . ." I thought I heard Mickey sigh. "Okay, the pertinent part of the story is that Rachel is somebody I just met and she's living with him and she wanted me to meet him." Mickey waited. He was staring at me. Waiting.

I started typing again. He wasn't going to let up. I knew him. Sure enough, he wasn't satisfied. "So, why are you so interested in him?"

"Who said I was?"

Then he laughed. "I say you are. You haven't told me the whole story, Charlie."

I sighed and pushed my chair back, then I looked around the room as if the place were bugged. Everybody was out. Warner stood up and made a noise when she yawned. "Okay, it's like this, but don't tell anybody."

Anybody but Mickey would have leaned forward, but being Mickey, he leaned back in his chair and waited. He had a cigar in his mouth. "Want one?" He threw me one and I lit it and blew smoke out and swung my knee-high boots up on my desk. "I feel funny telling you but I will."

So we puffed on our cigars and I told him about the baby. The rain was pouring down like crazy. Upstairs in what I called the executive suite, Mei, the Indonesian secretary, and Milli were frantically covering cracks in the wall and the space around the windows with masking tape. Elbert and John were out in Brooklyn, Bobby was in Jersey, Mas was at a Broadway location with Sharif, and Vinny was home with the flu.

"I can see how tempted she is. She's had a life of living on the edge."

"Like you, huh, Charlie?"

"Well, sometimes I've been worried. Let's leave it at that. If you're living in a different country and you're not close to any family and you're just out there . . . I know what that's like."

"So how much is he giving her to have the baby?"

"I don't know. I don't even know if it's really like that. She wants the baby. He wants the baby. It's only fair that he pays her expenses."

Mickey was silent. I could hear him thinking. Cigar smoke was graying up the office.

"Okay," I finally said when I'd puffed out a perfect ring and he still hadn't spoken. "Maybe he is paying her. In a way," I clarified. Silence. Lots of smoke. "She'll tell me. I'm sure she'll tell me. She tells me everything. More than I want to know."

"So why are you so surprised?"

"Because I kept hearing about this baby, baby, baby thing and how much it meant to her and how her marriage was damaged because of her husband not wanting one and I believe it. But when you throw in being taken care of for the rest of your life . . . when you throw money into the scenario . . . I just think maybe I don't know the whole story. What do you think?"

"I think I should have a fuckin' baby for this guy and quit this fuckin' job, that's what I think!"

I laughed. "Come on, Mickey, what do you really think?"

He grinned. "I think, Charlie Charlie, that you meet the real crazies. Your life is not normal. And neither—"

The door crashed open and Bobby, about six and a half feet of him, materialized. He was soaked with rain from his long blond curls down to his cowboy boots, which squished across the wooden floor. "Guess who just got arrested for drugs in Jersey?" he bellowed.

Warner got off her L.L.Bean cushion and bounded toward the wet giant. "The cousin of our pal at One Twenty-Four Canal!"

It was galvanizing news but there was no time to comment for suddenly the radio was squawking. Mas was saying, "Thirty-three to base. Thirty-three to base," and Mickey was striding through the room to stand in the open door for better reception. He stood there getting soaked from the blowing rain, shouting into the radio, "Five-oh to Three-three. Go ahead."

"One eighty-nine saw a delivery of watches at Eleven Sixty-One and we got the plate. New York Whiskey Charley George four seven two Charley."

I wrote it down and called, "I got that, Mickey."

Sheets of rain poured into the room; rain drummed on the air conditioner over the door like rain on a tin roof in the Caribbean.

"Did you get that, Five-oh?"

"Affirmative. Ten-four."

"He's headed for the Holland Tunnel."

"Stick with him."

The radio crackled and Mickey called, "Thirty-three? You're breaking up. Ten-five. Ten-five." Then when nothing but static came over the air, he slammed the door and came back into the room shaking rain off his jeans. Bobby dried his long hair with a towel, and Warner did one of her joyful little dances between him and her cushion. Bobby said, "Mas is prob'ly in the hole."

Then, as if suddenly remembering his news, Bobby was shouting, "Picked up for drugs in Jersey! And this guy is the son-in-law of the guy whose van was parked in front of that new location on Canal last Monday. What the fuck!" He tossed the towel on his desk and fumbled for a Marlboro. "Whaddya think, Mick?"

Mickey had pulled off his wet boots and was now leaning back in his chair. "What do I think? I think we're not paid enough to risk our fuckin' lives dealing with drugs. Get the fuckin' DEA in on this and leave me the fuck out of it."

It was mid-afternoon, after my take-out lunch from the Moroccan place, and I was wondering if I should walk to Poppy's for a Diet Coke to wake myself up. Just one more page and this surveillance report would be finished. I saved it and started typing again. I realized Mickey was making a personal call. I didn't want to listen, but we were alone, the radio wasn't that loud, and I couldn't help but hear.

"Bailey! Pick up! Okay, just listen then. I'm sorry I got so mad at you last night. It wasn't because you shit on the carpet. It's because you tried to hide it. You shit right next to the exercise bike and you know I never go over there. That's what made me mad. That you tried to hide it. So I'm sorry I kicked you outta bed last night. I'll be home in a few hours. I just wanted to say I'm sorry."

I never looked up. I didn't dare. If Mickey was smirking, if it had all been done for effect, I would not give him the satisfaction of a response. Not a flicker of an eyelash. I was doing my work. I would not look away from the computer screen. Was he putting me on? Waiting to catch my eye and grin? Was he counting the beats before I would look up?   Or   was this just something between a boy and his dog?

It was Saturday. I had Ivory-ed all my clothes in the bathtub to save the eight dollars I would have had to give the Turkish woman on Second Avenue. I carefully wrung out each sock, carried them across the room, and then laid them down flat one at a time. I imagined I was putting fish on a grill in some summer place like Capri instead of socks on a radiator in a walk-up on Lexington.

I thought of Rachel. I hadn't heard from her in two weeks and though I told myself I wasn't worried, I was uneasy. Robert answered the phone and said he'd give her the message that I had called, said that she was up in New Hampshire. Yes, that was it. Of course, she was.

And, of course, he didn't have anything to do with his wife's disappearance. Absolutely not.

I waved at the lions in front of the library on Fifth Avenue and went up the steps two and three at a time. A little research can be a dangerous thing, I thought, as I turned the handle and whirred through the yards of microfiche. November 2, 1950. Truman was president. A sale at Saks, one at B. Altman. I slowed down then started going backward slowly until I found the page.

FATAL FALL

Ridgefield, Conn, November 1.

THE DEATH OF Mrs. Seymour Durst was listed as an accident by Dr. Matthew Lange, assistant medical examiner of Fairfield County. Mrs. Durst fell off the roof of her home as firemen and policemen tried to rescue her with ladders.

Esther Weiss Durst, 32 years old, was the wife of Seymour Durst, real estate multi-millionaire. Dr. Lange said she had been receiving medication for allergies and while under the influence of sedatives had gone out onto the pitched roof from a bedroom window and then slipped on wet leaves.

Suicide? Maybe. I took the photocopy and jammed it into my canvas bag then went on to look up anything about Robert Durst.

It took hours. Saturday was not the day for this. Standing in line with my filled-out forms, waiting for someone to bring me microfiche for the right dates, waiting for a free machine, threading it, turning the handle until the date leapt into view, then finally reading the article. The only articles I found about Robert's father were about his charity work. And once he'd gotten involved in a congressional hearing regarding zoning and development. Rachel was right. He was a tycoon but rather quiet about it. He'd made the money himself. The father of three sons and a daughter and a widower all these forty-something years.

Then I found the article about Robert's wife, Kathleen. Suddenly there it was. I expected more but this was the *New York Times*, after all. It was odd that he had not reported her missing for four days. Some confusion about her return from a weekend. What had Rachel said? Weekends apart?

"Friends interviewed by police said they could not imagine that she would do anything to jeopardize her graduation in June."

Robert Durst was quoted as telling the police that they had had marital problems in the past but that recently everything had been fine between them. He could think of no reason why she would want to run away. On the morning of February first, Kathleen Durst had spoken to the doorman and walked out of the building on Riverside Drive. That was that. Never been seen again. It was a small piece. Not the least bit inflammatory. To me, the article screamed, *"Don't read this and if you do, don't get excited."*

I walked home slowly, letting bus after bus on Madison whoosh past me. In two hours, after I'd washed my hair and pulled on my black velvet suit, I was sitting across from Baron von Alvensleben at the Carlyle. An hour after that I was sitting across from him at Le Cirque. We talked about Geneva, about Gstaad, and people we knew. Andre had taken a chalet in Rougement; I knew that Catherine was just back from Paris. It was the best kind of Saturday night for me. A chance to lead my other life.

How many times can you reheat fried squid and still be happy about it? I peered through the little window of my oven at eye level and wondered. Then I took a step backward into the living room, bent down to open the half fridge the possible eight inches, and twisted my body to reach in for the white wine. It was lunchtime, a Sunday. I'd lived in Europe for years; I didn't brag about having a glass of wine with lunch in New York, but I refused to feel guilty either.

It was a day of melting snow, with gray slush in the gutters and a gunmetal sky pressing down over the bone-chilling cold. I glanced at the movie section of the *Times* and then tossed it on a chair. The coffee table was set with my silver which was a long-ago wedding present from Mother, a cloth napkin, and a wine glass. I served myself the squid and thought about a movie. I was getting paid so little I actually had to weigh the pros and cons of going. Was it worth nine dollars? Today? Or could I wait until it got to Fiftieth Street and Eighth Avenue and pay only three? Of course, if I paid nine dollars it would be in my neighborhood and I would walk there in five minutes and the cheap movie meant a dollar and a half each way on the bus and made the movie cost six dollars and with two buses in each direction it was a lot of time. Time was money, somebody said. My time? Earning twelve dollars an hour at Parker's? And only when I actually left the warehouse on assignment. No, my time wasn't money.

The phone rang. That husky voice said my name.

"Rachel! How are you?"

"I'm okay. Listen, do you want to come over tonight and cook something? I always come to you but Bob's away, and we'll have the place to ourselves."

When I didn't answer immediately, she seemed anxious. "I mean I want you to come. It'll be—"

"I'd love to. How are you?"

"I—" She sounded uncomfortable.

"Are you alone?" I asked.

"Yes, but," she sighed. "I don't know, I don't want to really talk now. I feel funny on this phone."

"Well, we'll talk tonight." Funny on that phone? What did that mean? "What shall I bring? Wine? A salad?"

We decided on red wine at seven and at seven I stepped into the elevator on Greene Street and pushed the top button. God, the place was huge. The grandiose square footage—square footage never to be taken lightly in Manhattan—hit me all over again. It seemed like miles of sleek shining wood floor.

Rachel was wound up as she checked the water boiling for the pasta, wound up as she chopped tomatoes and pushed them through a sieve. I watched her talk, eyes flashing, dark hair knotted back with two tortoise-shell clips, tendrils trailing over the black turtleneck. She was dramatic, full of fire and anxiety. Pent-up. She'd probably gone for a month without sex and then it was awful. I hated to think of checking into a hotel with someone you knew was—well, less than wonderful. No romance. All for that egg situation.

Finally we were at the table with wine glasses filled and pasta primavera steaming before us. "You know when you feel you don't belong? When you wonder where you are? When you feel off-balance and wonder what you want?" Rachel could carry on like this ad infinitum. Sometimes she appeared so young, so giddy, entirely scatty.

"Are you second-guessing the baby idea?"

She blinked and I realized I'd been far too off-hand. "No!" She appeared shocked. "That is what-what I know I want. It's the writing. It's-it's New Hampshire versus here. New York. It's . . ." She stopped.

"Are you writing here? Is it okay with Robert around? I have to call him Robert now. He is a Robert."

She nodded. "He's terrific. He's way down there." She tilted her head back toward the front door. "Usually all day. Computer, fax, phone." I could see a big red leather wing chair and a large carved wooden desk sitting on top of an Oriental rug. A standing lamp completed the tableau. It was an outpost, a stage-setting thirty yards away from the kitchen and the dining room table.

"It's amazing," I said. "This space. I suppose it's privacy and you don't hear each other but not having walls—say, where are the bedrooms?"

"I'll show you after dinner. There are walls but they don't reach the ceiling. There's a gap so I can hear him from his room to mine." She shook her head. "But what I was thinking about is this idea of really loving to be in New Hampshire. Getting so much done in complete privacy."

The phone rang and she leapt from the table "Oh, hi," her deep voice dropped even lower as she leaned against the butcher block island and twirled the cord of the wall phone around one index finger. "No, it's fine. Are you at a pay phone? Mmmm. Good for you. I have C here and we're just eating and drinking wine and talking about life in general." She listened. "Me, too! Oh, I wish you were. That would be really, really fun!" She laughed merrily.

I was listening, of course. Maybe I wasn't listening so much as hearing.

But listening is human nature, for Pete's sake. It's even animal nature. A dog would listen. Warner practically took notes in the office. I thought Rachel sounded so affectionate with him. This was a good thing. Maybe he did have his warm moments. Rachel was missing Robert or being quite a good actress. Telling him to call later to say good night. Sweet. Maybe the baby wasn't such a business deal after all.

"Yes, I love you." Her voice was a husky whisper but I heard it anyway. "Oh, I really love you."

Suddenly I knew it wasn't Robert.

I filled Mickey in. "The rest of the evening was just talk—about renovating her house in New Hampshire, about her family. Her father died when she was thirteen, and then her mother died the next year. Her mother left her some money. She has a sister somewhere, but they don't get along."

Mickey and I were alone in the office. He shook his head. "So she's all drippy on the phone with somebody, and she's supposed to be having a baby with Robert?"

"Sounds like that. I didn't ask her. She didn't tell me."

"Charlie, is she fucking this guy?"

"How do I know? It sounded like that kind of I've-made-love-to-you voice and it *is* the last decade of the twentieth century. People do go to bed together. Or so I hear." I sighed. I wondered if Mickey was in love with anybody. I wondered if he wondered about me. Sometimes the other men made remarks, which I fielded with a little smile or silence. I kept them at bay. Firmly. I liked to think I was dignified about it. Truth was that I loathed being celibate, but not being celibate took so much time and energy. Wardrobe-planning alone. And with whom would I not be celibate? Nobody. There was no one I loved.

The door slammed and Warner barked when Vinny, Bobby, and four other men walked in, taking up all the space in the area between our desks. With their jeans and their boots and their Stetsons and jean jackets, it was like a crowd scene from some Western. Except everybody had New York accents.

March was measured in wet socks drying on the radiator, and lost gloves. Then the snow melted in the gutters, and I no longer pulled on boots without thinking. There was the occasional day when we left the front door of the office open for an hour or so. Surveillance camera and security be damned.

Of course, this was unreasonable for Warner, who was terrified of every street noise, every squeal of brakes. A backfire was the signal that war had broken out. She shuddered, she shivered, she rolled her big brown eyes in terror. Warner, named after Warner Brothers, had been found in a counterfeit T-shirt raid in a dark and smelly basement in Queens. She had been in a cage with an empty water dish and two other boxer puppies slated to be teasers for dog fights. When they weren't being used for entertainment, the pit bulls were to guard drugs. The men rescued Warner, but the other puppies died. Warner's cruelty-filled days were still vivid to her. Poor neurotic Warner. We all loved her, but she was just another sign of the accepted lunacy that defined Parker's: an agoraphobic guard dog.

Rachel called in late March and we went to an art gallery opening and then climbed the stairs to my apartment. "Always love your paintings, books, being here," she said pulling off her black cape and shaking her long hair out of the newsboy cap.

"Open this." I handed her a bottle. "I'll get the cheese. I may not have bread, but I do have crackers. If you want anything else just go down to my kitchen."

"Down to your kitchen?"

"The deli downstairs. Open twenty-four hours a day."

"No, this is great." She poured white wine into our glasses. Amazing, I thought as I watched her talk. You just open a bottle and Rachel opens her mouth. And herself. Entirely. A great need to confide.

"I met him last summer. I didn't-didn't even like him at first. I found him to be very quiet, almost withdrawn. He's a painter. I'm always attracted to this type. My husband was an exception. I'm always attracted to the artists, the writers. Anyway, he's-he's very sensitive to me, to what I think about. We talk about things I can't imagine talking to anyone else about." She sighed and then reached for her wine.

"If he's in New Hampshire and you're here, when do you see him?"

She looked sheepish. "Well, he's come down here a couple of times when Bob's been-been away and I've gone up there. I was there for a couple of weeks the-the last time." I looked at her. "I know. I know. I'm-I'm being careful. Really we are."

Silence in the apartment except for the radiator's hiss.

"Are you in love with him?"

"Yes, I do love him. It keeps growing and growing." Her big dark eyes were bright in the candlelight. Rachel could look very Spanish at times.

"Isn't this all getting a bit complicated?"

She sighed and started to pull at a strand of hair.

"So are you going to go on trying to get pregnant and have the baby with Robert?"

"Oh, absolutely!"

"So you're making love to Robert in the middle of every month and you're making love to—what's his name, anyway?"

She shook her head and then she said, "Let's just call him Vermont."

I began again. "And you're being careful?" She nodded. "Does Vermont know about the plan with Robert?"

"I told-told him a few weeks ago. I didn't think it was fair not to."

I waited. "Well, what did he say?"

"Well, he's not happy about it. I didn't expect him to burst into song. I mean, he's-he accepts it. He knows I want a baby."

"Maybe he could get you pregnant and the three of you would be very happy." That's me. Fix everything. The last page of a novel. Tie it up in ribbons.

"His wife left him four-four years ago, and he doesn't want a baby. He feels that it's too-too much of a commitment."

I am thoroughly sick of that word. I think of being committed, I guess. Mental hospitals loom into view. It's like Mae West saying she believes in the institution of marriage but she isn't ready for an institution.

"So he's-he's cautious, wants more time. His wife probably hurt him. He might get over it."

I was thinking. "Yes. He might get over it and want a child with you in three months."

"I don't have three months!" Rachel said in exasperation. "My birthday is coming up and I'm still not pregnant. And Bobby wants a child. There is no guarantee that Vermont will ever want a-a child. I can't back away from this with Bobby. And besides," she hesitated. "I don't think I told you that I talked him into going to-to this fertility clinic. It's on Fifth Avenue. It's so expensive it's almost a joke. You would never imagine it's a clinic. You sit in this gorgeous living room and everybody speaks in whispers. I expected a butler to appear. Anyway, I think I'm okay. I've always thought that I'd be incredibly fertile. Having babies right and left. They think I'm okay." She sipped wine. "But Bob's sperm count is low."

"He's what? Over fifty?"

"Fifty-four. Age-age doesn't really matter but he's never gotten anyone pregnant before. Certainly not-not on purpose. And not by accident that-that he knows of. That bothers him."

"Why would his sperm count be low? Why would anybody's? Heredity? Junk food? Tight underwear?"

Rachel laughed a big husky horse-laugh. "They say it's stress. He's trying too-too hard." We both started laughing. "These-these doctors say that he has other signs of stress, too."

"Like what?"

Rachel was still laughing. "Like . . . like . . ." She put her hand over her mouth and tried to get the words out. "Like nail-biting and-and dandruff!" She honked with laughter. "Evidently they go with low sperm count!"

We both found it terribly funny. I poured the last of the wine a few minutes later and thought about getting up at five. I wouldn't be enticed into opening another bottle. Not for all the revelations in the northern hemisphere.

Rachel was very quiet suddenly. I asked her about the screenplay. We talked about it but she was distracted. "You're still thinking about Robert and getting pregnant, aren't you?

"On my mind constantly. Can't turn it off." She looked past me, past my Haitian paintings. I have to get pregnant. I have to have this baby."

"You will. It'll happen. But not necessarily this minute. Haven't you heard of couples who despair of having a child and the minute they bring home the adopted baby, the wife is suddenly pregnant? The pressure's off and suddenly—"

"I don't have the luxury of time. It's not only my birthday coming up. It's—"

"Does Robert know about Vermont?"

"I told him. He understands."

"He does?" I fairly squeaked in disbelief.

"Yeah. He's a great person. I want him as the father of my child. He and I have never wanted to be in love. We don't want all that. We have totally resisted the romantic idea. Bobby isn't jealous. He doesn't expect me to live like a nun. He knows about Vermont and the way I feel."

"This might very well unfold that you have Robert's baby and end up living with Vermont in New Hampshire." I winced but continued. "Have you thought about it? Has Robert brought it up? Has Vermont thought about your bringing Robert's baby with you if you ever end up living with him?"

I didn't wait for any answers but got up, walked to the frontier between living room and kitchen, opened the fridge, angled my arm awkwardly and grabbed another bottle of wine. This is very interesting, I thought. I can sleep when I'm dead.

* * *

"So tell Elbert exactly what she said," insisted Mickey.

"We were standing in his bedroom—she was showing me around while he was on the phone in the kitchen—and it was white, an abstract painting on the wall, a big double bed covered in a white duvet. But right where he would see it first thing in the morning when he opened his eyes was the only photograph in the entire huge loft. Blown up to about fifteen by eighteen. Maybe bigger. A black-and-white photo of a little girl standing on a beach wearing shorts and scowling at the camera. Blond curly hair and sun-tanned and cute."

Elbert and Mickey and Bobby were all quiet, all smoking, all listening. Warner yawned, then rearranged herself on her L.L.Bean cushion. "I said I didn't think Robert had any children, and Rachel said, 'Oh, he doesn't. That's this little girl he always thought of as his daughter. It's a really, really sad story.' I looked at her, and she dropped her voice and practically started whispering. She said that when Bobby was out in California he met the love of his life—before he was married—and they started living together and she told him a month later that she was pregnant by a former boyfriend. He said that was fine and stuck by her, the baby was born, and they were happy. But when the little girl was about four years old, the mother decided to leave him. He was very upset, didn't want her to go. Rachel said he was devastated. She left anyway and took the little girl and moved to Mexico. It was very sad for Bobby." I stopped. "Then Rachel said something strange." I took a deep breath. "She said that a year after that Bob went down to visit them in Mexico and had a good time but that a year after that visit, after he'd moved to New York, he contacted her parents for her address and they told him that their daughter and granddaughter had disappeared."

"Christ," said Elbert, pushing out a stub of a cigarette and preparing to light another.

"Rachel said—her exact words were—that the parents thought that they had been murdered." I waited. All three men stared at me. Then they were all, in unison, lighting up again. Three clicks of the three lighters. "I started to ask her another question, and she motioned for me not to.

Robert was off the phone, and she didn't want him to hear. The walls of the bedroom don't reach the ceiling so it's all open. You can hear."

"So that makes three people in this guy's life who have disappeared." Elbert was gazing into space through a cloud of smoke. Mickey was staring at Elbert, and Bobby was staring at me.

"The love of his life. Before the wife. I think Rachel said she was somebody he met when he was getting his master's degree."

"What do you think?" asked Mickey, directing his question to Elbert, who had the psychology degree.

"What do I think?" responded Elbert. "I think our fucking heir apparent to the fucking real estate empire has a full-blown fucking problem with women who want to leave him, that's what I think."

The phone rang and Bobby picked up. "For Elbert? Okay. I'll tell him. Thanks, Mei." He hung up. "Joe O'Connor wants to see you. He's coming in about five minutes to pick up something."

"Christ. I have to find it and get it photocopied. I'll be upstairs." He put the cigarette in his mouth and grabbed his jacket and hurried out. The door slammed and then we heard him open the next door and clump with his boots up the wooden stairs.

"C," said Bobby, "I 'd stay away from this fuckin' guy. I know you like Rachel, but this can't be a coincidence. What the fuck does your friend see in him?"

Mickey looked at me and I looked back at him and didn't answer. He was the only one I'd told about the baby, but he'd never talk. "She thinks he is a wonderful person. At least that's what she tells me. She's known him for ten years. Thinks he's great."

"I've heard enough," said Mickey picking up the phone. He punched in a number, waited, and then said, "Lemme have the Missing Persons Squad."

At eight o'clock the next morning I went to One Police Plaza. I signed in and was given the I.D. check and a pass, was scanned with a metal detector, and then I rose in an elevator. The doors opened into an enormous room filled with rows of desks and men in shirt sleeves, some in uniforms, hurrying between them; phones were ringing.

Detective Frank Martinez was slender, trim, tall. He wore a white shirt and tie, was in plain clothes. He had a strong, handsome face. It was narrow but with a wide, clear forehead. He had high cheekbones, black hair, and very kind brown eyes.

The men at Parker's had taken me seriously but would the senior officer of the Cold Case Squad of the NYPD? Or would I be treated politely and then ushered out with a "We'll be in touch"?

"I looked over the files after the call yesterday." His desk was covered in manila folders. "Everyone thought he had killed his wife, but there was no body, no witness, and supposedly she was seen in Manhattan the day after he said he put her on the train in North Salem." He sighed. "My predecessor handled the case. They never arrested Durst and old Seymour had him lawyered up immediately. All top lawyers. They said to call them if we had anything. We couldn't get near him, though everybody was sure he was involved."

I told him about meeting Rachel, about her trying to have a baby with Robert Durst. "Is she pregnant?"

"Not yet," I said. "But she hopes to be any minute."

We went over what we knew: Kathleen Durst was twenty-nine years old and a fourth-year medical student at Albert Einstein when she disappeared on February 1, 1982. She called the school and said she was ill and would not be coming in. Later that morning she left the Riverside Drive co-op building she lived in. The superintendent and the doorman were the last to see her.

"But did she make that call to the school?" I asked. "Or did someone else?"

Detective Martinez said, "We don't know. And we don't know if the super and the doorman saw her or a woman who looked like her. Durst swore he took her to the train station the night before but no one saw him with her; no one saw her on the train."

"Makes no sense to me that he waited four days to report her missing."

"Makes no sense to anybody. He said he wasn't worried because she often stayed with friends. Every one of her friends said there was no way she would run away before graduation. She'd worked so hard, was looking forward to it. June. So close." The detective paused. "There was no activity on her credit cards." He appeared to switch gears. "Tell me more about Rachel. How did she meet Durst?"

"She said she met him ten years ago at a party but the timing was all wrong. It wasn't a great love affair. Very short-lived. Rachel said her life and his were complicated and that his wife had disappeared a few years before. She was casual about that, and I was just getting to know her. Had no idea she was living with Robert Durst."

Detective Martinez was silent, attentive. I went on. "When I remarked that her disappearance must have been a shattering experience, she sort of shrugged and said they were separated at the time. Then Rachel got married and eight years later that was over and she met Robert again. They both regretted not having a child."

Phones were ringing, people were rushing back and forth but I was with this detective, on an island, telling this story. "She said that lawyers were consulted, papers were drawn up. It's all in black and white. She will have the child and be the primary caregiver and, in return, she and the child will be taken care of forever."

Detective Martinez was silent, listening, and I continued. "She came to New York and didn't have a place to live, and he has this huge loft with two bedrooms." I stopped then remembered one late-night conversation. "He also has an ex-girlfriend who visits once in a while. Maybe Robert is getting involved with her again. She is a very tough blonde real estate agent, and Rachel doesn't like her, and she doesn't like Rachel."

"Does she know about this arrangement with the baby?"

"Rachel says Robert is not telling anyone, and she trusts him not to, so the answer is no."

"She trusts him?"

"Well, yes, she says she does."

There were files nearly a foot high on his desk between us. The little tabs on the edges were like tongues; every one was labelled Durst. Detective Martinez shook his head. "He got away with it."

I told him about the photograph of the little girl on the wall in the bedroom. He shook his head again, looking sad.

I was staring at the files and said I'd love to take a look, and he said, "Can't let you do that, but I think I'll go to the men's room, and I'll cough on my way back." With one quick movement he turned the stack around and pushed it toward me, then stood up and left.

The pile was so high I had to stand up. I flipped the top manila file open and saw the names and addresses of Kathleen's family. I skimmed page after page. The cough. Files slammed closed. I sat down. He sat down.

The detective was attentive to every word, and I felt comfortable telling him that I worried that Rachel would be in danger once she did produce a child. "She's big-boned and dark and sort of an expansive earth-mother figure and Kathleen was blonde and thin and WASP-y. Plus that real estate agent is another thin, petite blonde, and I don't think he will need or want Rachel around once he has the child."

Detective Martinez nodded. "He's Jewish, she's Jewish, so the child will be, but, after that, I'm afraid you're right. He won't need Rachel."

I sighed. "Father and mother are both dead, and she has a sister she hasn't seen in years. If she disappeared, I'm not sure who would know about it."

We agreed that I was to keep my eyes and ears open but I would not, of course, voice any fears to Rachel. I could imagine her telling Robert how silly I was to think he'd killed his wife.

Detective Martinez said he was going to reexamine the case notes. Meanwhile, I would continue to be the confidante. He gave me his business card and said, "Call me anytime, day or night."

As I walked out into the sunlight, I felt more worried than ever because the danger had been confirmed. But I also felt relieved because now there was someone else in charge.

Back in the warehouse I told the men how it had gone, leaving out the baby. "This Frank Martinez was so cool, so sensitive, so intelligent. I like him. A lot."

"Who is he? Who'd you talk to?" barked Vinny.

"Detective Martinez. He is a senior officer of the Cold Case Squad which is part of the Missing Persons Squad. They get sixteen thousand reports of missing New Yorkers every year. That's for twenty-two investigators to find. That is . . ." I picked up a pencil and scrawled on my desk calendar in between the crescents of coffee stains. "That's about seven hundred and twenty-seven people for each investigator to find in a year. About two lost people every single day."

"So Charlie, are you gonna find her or not?" asked Mickey.

What a pain he could be. I put my feet up on my desk and leaned back in the chair, thinking about Frank Martinez. "He told me they never close a missing-persons case. Remember Ethan Patz? That little boy disappeared in 1979. Still open. They never close it unless it is reassigned as a homicide."

"What do you see in Rachel, C?" asked Bobby.

"It's her vitality. Her spirit. She's lived all over, had to take care of herself. Says she doesn't have friends in New York to talk to. She's younger than I am. I feel protective. And I like her passion."

Bobby snorted. "Well, I hope her passion doesn't just get her disappeared." He went back to his little hand-held computer puzzle, and Mickey shook his head. Then Warner went crazy with barking and jumping around. The doorbell was ringing next door. Then somebody upstairs buzzed the door open. Then the scam phone started ringing.

I grabbed it, knowing the men would never answer it, and tried an English accent. "Global." I listened. "No, I'm afraid you have the wrong number. No. There's no Samantha here. Goodbye." I hung up, then clapped my hand to my forehead. *Damn.* I had been Samantha last week. On Broadway. Mickey guessed immediately what I'd done. "Another identity crisis, Charlie?" I could hear the smirk. It was a serious smirk, bordering on a grin that could break into a laugh. I refused to look at him.

"So I said, 'Listen, let's just talk-talk about it.'" Rachel looked as if she were dying to smoke, but she didn't smoke. It was her hand gestures, the way she put her thumb and forefinger up to the corners of her mouth as if measuring the distance.

"You think he's changed his mind?" I asked, taking a sliver of brie. From the side, of course. Never cut the point off; the French were fanatical about it. Bad luck, bad manners, wildly bad form. I looked down and thought, *For Pete's sake, don't tell her.*

"I don't know. He's backing-backing away. He is trying to decide where he wants to live. He is getting out of the family business and doesn't-doesn't really know what he wants. Plus, he's going out more and more with that real estate agent. You know the-the blonde with the tough voice?"

Funny how two brunettes could mention "a blonde" and immediately picture the enemy. "What's she like?" I reached for a cracker.

"Hard as nails. Course she knows all-all about his family. Out for the bucks."

"Where'd you meet her? In the loft?"

"Yeah, she came over one night and, of course, I was there washing the dinner dishes. She took one look—one look like she had food poisoning and practically said to Bob, 'Who's that? The maid?'"

I burst out laughing. "Oh, Rachel! She didn't!"

"Practically!" Her dark eyes flashed and I thought she resembled Anna Magnani.

"Well, if she's dating him and she finds out he's living with somebody it's bound to be a little surprise. I mean, I'm not on her side, but can you blame her?"

Rachel shrugged and took a gulp of wine. "I made-made sure that Bobby didn't tell her about the plan. The-the baby."

"You told me that but are you sure he won't?" I thought of someone falling in love with Robert and wanting to marry him and suddenly discovering that he had an agreement with a woman to bear his child. Might prove awkward. And, of course, she would want to be the mother of his child and then there'd be a race to see which woman could get pregnant first.

"No, he won't. I trust Bobby in a lot of ways I haven't trusted anyone before. He is an unusual person."

We talked until nearly midnight, Rachel emptied the bottle as she had so many evenings before, and then clunked down the stairs to go back to Greene Street.

I lay awake in the sleeping bag and wondered how many people got away with murder. Accidents, suicides—maybe thousands of them were really murder. Toss in disappearances. Elbert had surprised me in the office by shouting, "You are just like Grace Kelly in *Rear Window*! You won't stop until you're in his bedroom and he's coming at you!" Mickey and I had laughed. I grinned now thinking of it. Then I turned on my side with my elbow banging loudly on the wooden floor, which was a sleeping-bag hazard. I fell asleep thinking of me and Mickey laughing.

There was always a lot happening at work. The room was noisy with arguments, theories, plans. There were usually at least three or four of us in the downstairs office, sometimes as many as a dozen, with ex-cops coming and going. There were four desks jammed in, five chairs on casters, bags of counterfeit goods waiting to be sorted and put in the back, sledgehammers hanging on one wall, Wanted posters on another. Warner lolled on her L.L.Bean cushion on the floor near Bobby. Everybody had their feet up, cowboy boots on the desks, cleaning their guns, listening to Trisha Yearwood. I was the only female, unless you counted Warner.

Vinny talked about starting a security service on Staten Island for people who had died. More specifically, guards for the houses of people who had to go to funerals. Burglars supposedly read the obits, knew when the houses would be empty, and would strike in broad daylight, cleaning them out. I thought it was ridiculous, but everyone else thought it was genius. I shook my head. Who knew what went on in Staten Island? The guard service never materialized.

Another afternoon somebody thought we could sell real jeans overseas for an enormous profit. Sharif, the Mauritanian, would translate for Africa because he spoke French and Arabic. We knew customs, duties, how all that worked. The men were pretty geared up about it, and then the radio crackled with a location on Canal Street, and we all grabbed jackets, radios, and keys and stampeded out. The export business vaporized with the slamming of the warehouse door.

I wrote Frank Martinez a letter thanking him for seeing me and expressing surprise that he wasn't a gruff, hard-boiled cynic. I told him I was mystified as to why Kathleen's family had not kept in contact with the NYPD the way Ethan Patz's parents had and wondered if the Durst family or Robert himself had put pressure on them to back off. How could you, if your daughter or your sister disappeared?

That same afternoon Rachel called. I knew she preferred my apartment to anywhere else, so I told her to come at seven. "I'm broke. Stone-dead-flat-out-wondering-if-I-could-sell-my-body broke," I said, and she laughed one of her big honking ones. "But you are always welcome." She offered to bring wine and cheese. I had a half-full box of crackers for us.

This is good, I decided, as it would have been one of those nights spreading Dijon mustard on Carr's water crackers. With one glass of wine. By candlelight, of course. A sense of ceremony was never to be neglected.

Rachel arrived wearing her big black cape, which she yanked off and draped over my desk chair. Her dark hair was wild and her eyes bright. We opened the wine and laid out the cheese on a wooden tray from Haiti. "I'm going crazy," she moaned. "*In*-sane."

"Robert?" I took a sip of wine.

71

"Yes, of course! But let's talk about you! How is your world?"

"Well, let's see. There's so much counterfeiting going on in Atlanta that Elbert thinks we should have a presence down there instead of depending on someone fairly unreliable called Chowderhead who screws up eighty-five percent of the time. Any day he's going to be arrested. He won't do us any good at all in the slammer, so today Elbert asked me if I would go to live in Atlanta."

"What did you say?"

"I told him I'd rather eat razor blades."

A great snort of laughter. "Good for you. You escaped the South. Don't go back!"

"All the fun is up here. Besides, what would I do without Mickey?"

"Mickey. Is he the one you described as looking like James Dean if James Dean hadn't slept in three years?"

I nodded. "He was telling me today about the Chinatown raid yesterday when they had to careen up on the sidewalk, and Rolexes were flying in every direction, and people were running, and Elbert in his new boots leapt out of the car and slammed the door. Then he disappeared. Mickey thought, my God, where'd he go? Elbert had slammed the door on his shoelaces and crashed facedown on the sidewalk."

We started laughing.

"Last week, we were waiting for the cops to do the seizure on Canal and we were all out of the vehicles waiting, waiting, waiting. None of us knew how to blend in or what to do. I went over to this vendor and bought a banana. I was eating it, walking along trying to look like a tourist from Omaha. Two minutes later I turned around and saw Mickey, Mas, Vinny, Bobby, Elbert—all of 'em wandering around eating bananas!"

Rachel was laughing. "You have adventures. I love that about your life."

"I do, too. Most of the people in my life I tell stories to. About the past, of how I feel, of what I believe, of what I want, but this is action."

Rachel looked a bit sad in the candlelight, and I felt sorry I'd said that last thing. "What are you thinking about?" I asked her.

"I hate to sound like a broken record, but I have to get pregnant. I-I haven't told you what this really means. Bobby is—he's going to take care of me for the rest of my life." She stopped and I waited.

When she didn't continue, I said, "I sort of assumed that if he would take care of the child and you are the child's mother..."

Rachel took a big gulp of wine as if fortifying herself. "It's-it's more than that. He's going to give me an office building."

My jaw dropped.

Rachel added, her voice excited. "On Lexington."

"My God," I managed.

"I can buy a house anywhere in the world. Or several. I can travel first class. Always. The best-best hotels. The best of everything. I will never-never worry about money again." Her eyes were bright. "I can do-do anything I want for the rest of my life!"

So this was it. I'd always felt she was holding something back. "I feel relieved talking about it. There's no one but you who would understand. One minute I'm so excited I could explode and the-the next I'm panicked about Bob's sperm count." She took another gulp of wine. "He has no sperm, you know. We are thinking of donor sperm."

"Really? That would be okay with him?"

"Yes. As long as no one ever knows. His name-name would be on the birth certificate and no one could ever know. It would be disastrous if they-they found out. Really disastrous." She emphasized the *really*.

We both reached for our wine glasses at the same time.

"Rachel, I have to say something." I paused. I thought of Martinez but couldn't stop myself.

"What? What?"

"I'm worried about you. Being with him, living with him. This arrangement..."

"Don't get all moral on me," she said on the verge of anger.

"I'm not. I'm worried about you. Look, his wife disappeared. Lots of people think he was involved. I confess, I went and read about it. And then there is the little girl and the former girlfriend who went to Mexico and disappeared."

"Oh, that was just a coin-coincidence."

"She left him. You said he was devastated."

"Oh, he was—he was upset but not devastated. It wasn't that serious. Maybe I gave you the wrong idea!"

"From a psychological point of view, he's been deeply damaged. His mother. You told me that he saw her fall. Now I know it was from the roof. Accident or suicide? Doesn't matter. He saw her die and he was what? Six years old? The lesson from that might be 'If you left me, then so will everyone else,' and that's too painful to bear, so if they want to leave, he . . ."

"No, he-he isn't like that! After his wife left he hired detectives, and he went around to-to hospitals looking for anyone with amnesia. He really tried to find her." She stopped. "Hey, I know he's strange. I mean, he's-he's never unwrapped his Christmas presents."

"I just don't want you to have a baby and disappear because he doesn't need you anymore or because you would be leaving him to be with somebody else."

"No, no! That-that won't happen! He's really not like that!"

"Okay. I just wanted you to know what I think, wanted to lay it out there. I worry about you. He's got a bad track record. Rachel, you're a journalist. Think about it. Doesn't it bother you that the significant women in his life have bad things happen to them?" *Like death.*

"Bob's had a hard time," she said, reaching for the tray of cheese. She wouldn't look at me.

"He's had a hard time but—"

"Yes, he has. And I'm going to be his good luck." She looked up at me as if daring me to argue. "The plan now is that I'll be artificially inseminated once a month until I'm pregnant." She laughed. "No more suites at the Plaza!" She popped a cracker in her mouth and chewed. "He wants an heir and I'll give him one. My God, think of the reward! I can do anything I want for the rest of my life! Have anything I want! Be-be anywhere I want!"

She laughed again. "Cici, the money is endless!"

The apartment was warm, the white wine was cold, and Rachel drank even more than usual. "You know," she said between quick sips. "Bob's father is leaving all his money to his grandchildren, skipping his own kids." I was wide-eyed but silent.

After she'd gone, I washed the wine glasses then settled myself in the bag. The rain was beating against the skylights, and I felt happy to be on the top floor, happy to hear the rain, happy to live alone. A pang of fear shot through me. Rachel was living with a man who'd done away with his wife. She was playing a rough game. Playing for keeps with a small, powerful man. He'd outmaneuver her and—what? I didn't know. *I have to get up in four hours*, I thought, telling myself to sleep. I zipped the bag right up to the top. I felt safe, but Rachel wasn't. *I have to get through to her. 'Forget the baby. Forget the money. Get away from Robert Durst.'*

I went to see Detective Frank Martinez a second time. He looked as surprised at what I had to tell him as I had been when I heard it. "An office building?" he echoed. "Can you imagine the rent coming in every month? It's a fortune!"

"Speaking of fortunes, Seymour Durst is leaving all his money to his grandchildren and—"

The detective finished the sentence for me. "And Robert is the only one with no kids."

A few days later Rachel called me at the office and said breathlessly into the phone, "I'm dying! Just got my period!" I started to speak, but she said that she couldn't talk, that she was in the loft and hung up. I heard the dial tone and replaced the receiver.

My misgivings had no effect on her. Could you be a naïve kid at thirty-eight? She was fey and delicate, ethereal and vulnerable, even as she stood with heavy boots, tall, big-breasted with that deep voice. I felt much older, even wiser, though, yes, I have been accused of being naïve, of living for the moment, of living on the edge. But I always consider the source of those opinions and decide that their standards are so far removed from mine that there is no validity to them whatsoever. Should a private detective give a second's thought to what an investment banker thinks of her life? Being the practical one in any relationship was a new dynamic for me.

This has to be Robert's fault. She looked as if she could produce triplets after a one-night stand. Fertile, fecund. There was a lushness to Rachel under the cloak, the loose tunics, and the long skirts that she layered, black on black.

Meanwhile the work at Parker's went on. I was down in Chinatown a lot. Another country on the island of Manhattan, and we were foreign. We didn't belong there. The population didn't cooperate with the police and only recently had the NYPD produced an officer who spoke their languages. I thought this was good but had heard that they thought of him as a traitor, so they wouldn't deal with him either.

I stared at the sketches of our perps on the office wall over Mickey's desk until I was blind. Mas was good at this, the rest of us getting better. I thought about blacks and whites and all the old racist clichés about looking alike. I could tell the Koreans from the Chinese and the Vietnamese from everybody else. The Koreans and the Vietnamese had taken over the area in the last few years. Little Italy was shrinking block by block as the Italians were squeezed out by the influx of Asians.

A Wednesday on Canal Street. "Think it's true, Mickey, that there are tunnels under Chinatown?"

"Maybe. Elbert thinks so."

"Then maybe we'll sit here until the Fourth of July and Kim won't ever show because he's just popped his head out of a hole in the sidewalk fifty-five blocks uptown. Like a little prairie dog."

"There he is!" Mickey grabbed the radio as we watched Kim in his khaki windbreaker wait to cross Broadway. It had taken only a second for the door behind him to open and close. "Bobby, subject is crossing toward the lot. If he pulls out to the right, you take him. To the left, I'll take him."

"Affirmative," came Bobby's voice.

"Three-three, move over to—"

Mas's voice came on the radio. "I'm behind you, Five-oh."

Mickey glanced in the rearview mirror then put the radio on the seat between us. I downed the last of my Diet Coke and, with eyes never leaving the subject crossing the parking lot, stuffed the can in a paper bag and tossed it in the back seat. I watched, like a slow-motion film, Kim stopping at a car, reaching into his trouser pocket for the key, putting the key in the door, the turn of the key, the opening of the door. Kim got in and slammed the door. We waited until he'd pulled forward and turned to the left. With two cars between him and us at the light, only then did we move. We were made within minutes—he saw us—within eight blocks of where it had begun. I won't go into all the details: the eerie silence that accompanied the quick turns, the speeding up a one-way street the wrong way, the cut-off through a parking lot, the catching the yellow light a millisecond before it went red, and that honking that seemed intrusive and silly and made no difference to us. My fingers were spread, pressing down on my thighs, and I was sure I could taste the adrenalin. You've never really lived until you've experienced a car chase in Chinatown.

The beginning of spring meant that the number of pigeons on the sidewalk was multiplied by a thousand and I stopped wearing gloves. The hookers came back, freshly resplendent in their theatrical outfits of boots, hot pants, and feathers. The girls looked cheaply glamourous until you got close enough to see the goosebumps. The days were getting longer. Getting up at five wasn't as horrible as it had been in the darkness of December and sometimes I actually made it home in daylight.

* * *

One morning in May, Mickey waved the *Daily News* in my face, then read aloud, "Seymour B. Durst, Real-Estate Developer Who Led Growth on West Side, Dies at Eighty-One."

I gasped.

The phone rang and Mas picked up. "Charlie! For you!"

Rachel's deep voice was solemn. "It's over. Bobby was at the hospital last night."

"I'm so sorry" came out of my mouth automatically. *Sorry he died before you got pregnant.*

"He's moving to California and I'm-I'm leaving New York."

"What? Now? Rachel, are you sure?"

Hearing her name, Mickey shushed everyone. The room went silent.

"Yes, he's closing the loft. I can't talk. He's here."

I hung up and was immediately assaulted with questions. Mickey and I exchanged glances. "Rachel is leaving New York and Robert Durst is moving to California. Alert the media." The men laughed, and Warner shook herself. Her collar jingled.

Mickey read off the locations west of Broadway, and I scrawled them down in my notebook. Mas grabbed a radio, and I slammed the door behind us. The day began.

May was the month of endings. The death of Seymour Durst ended the baby project, and Parker's was on life-support. The phones were cut off. Moby Dick got impounded, and we had no money to spring it. Our paychecks were bouncing. I think the IRS administered the coup de grace.

Both Rachel and Robert disappeared from my life.

Epilogue

The next year Rachel called and told me she had married Vermont and was pregnant.

A big white-shoe, risk-consulting firm offered me more than four times what Parker's had paid me—when they'd paid me.

Detective Frank Martinez and I kept in touch, both of us convinced that Robert Durst had orchestrated the disappearance and probable murder of his wife, Kathleen.

Robert married the blonde realtor in 2000, but went off to Galveston, Texas, and living as a mute woman, with wig and all, murdered his neighbor. Though he admitted killing and dismembering poor Morris Black, he claimed self-defense, and the jury ruled in his favor.

In 2010, the movie *All Good Things*, about Kathleen's disappearance, stirred interest in legal circles, as Durst had made several self-incriminating remarks to the producer. Westchester County District Attorney Jeanine Pirro decided to take another look at the 1982 missing-persons case.

In 2015, Robert Durst was the subject of the HBO documentary *The Jinx*. In the last segment, Durst goes into a bathroom, unaware that his mike is still live. It recorded him whispering to himself: "What the hell did I do? Killed them all, of course!"

In 2018, a Los Angeles judge ordered Durst to stand trial for the murder of his longtime friend and confidante Susan Berman, who was shot in the back of the head in December 2000. Berman had been scheduled to speak with police later that day about the disappearance of Kathleen Durst.

Bobby, as Rachel called him, sued his siblings for a share of the $4.4 billion family fortune and they settled with him for $65 million. He can afford the best legal minds once again.

Awaiting trial in a Los Angeles jail, I wonder what he thinks about. Maybe, after all those murders, Greene Street and the baby project are less vivid to him than my evening on a balcony in Santo Domingo is to me.

BODIES ALL OVER THE PLACE

Canal Street subway station. I made my way up the steps behind an Asian with a telltale black garbage bag full of product. From the shape I could tell it was handbags. Ten to one it's counterfeit, I thought.

A bitter day in February. I could have sworn that Chinatown was the coldest spot in Manhattan in winter and the hottest in summer. *Makes no sense*, I thought, as I threaded my way through the crowd of tourists and vendors calling, "Handbag! Fendi! Chanel! What you want? Have all!" Vietnamese were hawking watches, which were pictured on cardboard signs large enough to attract attention but small enough to tuck under a parka if a cop materialized. Africans were in on it, too, I noted. It was all pretty open. We at Parker's were always going after the big fish, the suppliers, not the little street guys.

I tuned it all out. Mickey had sent me down to check on a few locations. Easy. No buys. No conversation. Just a fly-by on foot. I could see my breath and even though it was only ten o'clock in the morning it was cloudy and darkish.

I was walking south on Lafayette looking for the address when I saw the police cars, red lights flashing. There was the EMS vehicle parked nearby. Cops all over. A ratty little park seemed to be the crime scene with a dozen cops standing around. I stayed away but when the trench-coated detectives moved aside, I could see the body of a man on a park bench.

Black trousers, gray parka falling open, some dark hair but going bald. Two men moved in with a stretcher and that big, ominous black bag. Someone else was running toward the scene with the yellow tape.

I turned away and called Mickey. "Are you on the radio now? There's a murder. Well, maybe not a murder, but there's a dead body down here."

"What's your location?"

"On Lafayette walking south. He's on a park bench. A lot of cops, EMS is here taking him away."

"Nothing on the scanner. A fire in Harlem, a robbery in midtown. Nothing else really."

"That's a surprise. Listen, I don't think that number on Lafayette is right. It's a jewelry store. No handbags, no watches. At least they aren't advertising it."

"See what you can find out."

"Okay."

We hung up. I retraced my steps and went in, had a little conversation about a birthday present for my sister, and chatted about the climbing price of gold. I looked around, asked about designer watches, but the watches I was shown were the right price, the real deal. I thanked the woman and deemed the place legit.

Out again in the cold. I pulled on gloves and started walking east on the periphery of the park. All the activity of twenty minutes before had evaporated. The park bench was empty; the cops were gone; there was no yellow tape. But up ahead, I saw red flashing lights, another EMS vehicle, more cops!

"Mickey! There's another dead body! It's behind a park bench in the leaves and the place is crawling with law enforcement!"

"Nothing on the radio. I went out for a sandwich, so maybe I missed it. Did you see the body?"

"Yes! Well, not this time. I can see it's a man. But the first time I got a good look. Male, late forties, a little patch of dark hair. He was lying down so I couldn't guess height or weight."

"Yeah, Charlie. Dead. Lying down. Good."

"Okay, okay. Well, you're not here. It's awful. Two dead bodies in one morning! I'm going to get something to eat and then do that last location."

"I can tell you're so upset it's affected your appetite."

"Oh!" I said in exasperation and hung up.

I did the last location, had a chocolate glazed doughnut and a Diet Coke and got warm again. I left the cafe and saw a dozen cops swarming between police cars and the EMS vehicle. They had the stretcher out. "Mickey!" I blurted into my cell. "There's another body! Another one! I can't believe it!"

"What's your location, Charlie?"

"I'm on the other side of that same little scruffy park. I guess I'm closest to Center Street."

"Nothing on the radio."

"There are bodies all over the place! What do you think this is? A serial killer? A spree killer?" I was breathless. I could hear Mickey turning up the scanner; there was a lot of static and then a barking voice, but I couldn't understand the words.

"Try to get closer, Charlie, and ask one of the cops."

"Okay. Wow, this is ama—" I stopped in mid-word as the crowd parted. Another body on a park bench. All I could see was dark trousers, gray parka. The tall detective in the trench coat bending over him stood up.

It was Detective Lenny Briscoe, a.k.a. Jerry Ohrbach. *Law & Order* did this sort of thing very well.

"You there, Charlie?"

"Yeah. I'll see you in a while."

I smiled all the way to the subway.

COURTROOM AS THEATER

As a private detective, I'm hired for the defense. I meet with the accused, again and again. I spend all day with them if they're out on bail; I spend hours in prison visiting rooms if they're not. And I go to court with them.

These are people admitting to despicable acts, people driven by desperation, by lust, by greed. Making decisions of stunning stupidity and now explaining themselves in public. A jury of "your peers" can be twelve people who look as if they are sleeping but who hold your life, or years of it, in their hands. Trial lawyers perform, often possess star power and know how to steal a show. The accused are the famous, the infamous, and the ordinary. The person who's made a terrible mistake now paraded before us in the theater of a courtroom. Human beings describing the worst day of their lives. All the drama one could ever imagine.

The first trial I remember was with Mother in Mississippi. We were doing an errand in a little town with a bronze Confederate war hero on a horse in the middle of the main drag. I can't think why we were there unless it was to buy udder cream from a farm-supply store. Mary the maid had told us it was why her skin was so perfect.

Writers always mention one-stoplight towns, but I'm not sure this place had even one. There was a courthouse with wide, white steps and, of course, a Mississippi flag. As one, we decided to park and go in. I thought we'd see an impressive courtroom, what I then regarded as empty pews, and maybe some elaborate woodwork, but instead the lobby was abuzz.

I asked what was going on, and a sweaty, red-faced man wearing a cowboy hat looked at me and stated, "Murder trial. He did it."

Mother slowly edged the big heavy door open and I followed her in. I remember the hush, the smell of wood, the sensation of being in church, which was quickly dispelled by the testimony. The judge asked someone to bring in the evidence. A self-important khaki-clad deputy strode in carrying two big paper bags, one in each hand, each bag bearing the large red Jitney Jungle logo. The Jitney Jungle was a grocery store in Mississippi.

We had to leave just after the black bra and the spattered-with-blood T-shirt were removed from the first bag. Now I am aghast at the flawed chain of evidence, but then all I could think of was *Couldn't they find a couple of plain paper bags?*

My first summer in London I started going to the Old Bailey. I was seduced forever by the wigs, the language, the sense of ceremony. The witness in the box described hearing the *bonk, bonk, bonk* on the stairs in the middle of the night. He kept repeating the noise, "Bonk, bonk, bonk." Only later would he realize it was the murderer dragging the body down to the first floor with the head hitting every step.

Mother would go anywhere just for the kick of it. It was a summer day in 1967, when those convicted in the murders of the three civil rights workers in June 1964, were to be sentenced. I was reading the paper. "Mother, it's this morning!"

The triple murder of Andrew Goodman, Michael Schwerner, and James Chaney was one of the most notorious crimes of the civil rights era but the state of Mississippi never charged anyone.. How well I remembered people laughing and joking about where the bodies were buried. It was on the news, in the newspapers, and lots of people said, "Them Yankees got what they deserved!" In those days the killing of a black man in Mississippi wasn't really talked about, so the state let it go. But the federal government indicted Sheriff Lawrence Rainey and his deputy sheriff, Cecil Price, and sixteen others for conspiring to deny the victims their civil rights. Rainey was acquitted, but Price and five others were convicted and were now to be sentenced. .

Mother and I jumped into the car and sped downtown; in half an hour we were standing in the crowd in front of the federal courthouse. I said, "Mother, the place is packed! We'll never get in!" She nodded, and then I saw her moving forward between people on the sidewalk. Mother was tall and I watched her progress; in minutes she was edging up the steps. *If she can, so can I* went through my mind. I did my own squeezing between elbows and pocketbooks and copped a spot in the very back of the courtroom pressed against the wall.

Those men from Neshoba County were a sorry-looking bunch. Sheriff Rainey and Deputy Sheriff Price were up in front, standing out in their khaki uniforms. The sheriff's mouth was stuffed with his usual Red Man chewing tobacco, his jaw moving. His belly protruded. All the men's faces looked blank and ignorant.

Mother was in the front row, sitting with the wives and girlfriends from Neshoba County. Their hair was ratted so high it could have gotten caught in ceiling fans; they wore white patent leather spike heels, swimming-pool-blue eye shadow, frosted pink lipstick, and pastel polyester. Mother said she had asked two to make room for her and they did. Then she opened a pack of Juicy Fruit and chewed all five sticks. "Just to fit in," she told me.

Sheriff Rainey, a Klansman, had been acquitted of the federal charges, as he was said to have been visiting his wife in the hospital in Meridian when the three young men were abducted and killed. The longest sentence, ten years, went to a Klan leader and one other. Cecil Price, also a Klansman, was sentenced to six years and served four and a half years in a federal penitentiary in Minnesota. He came back to Mississippi afterward and died at age fifty-three after falling from a cherry picker. Rainey was a folk hero to a lot of white people, but his career in law enforcement was over. He was given presents, people often broke into applause when they saw him, and he was asked to endorse everything from chewing tobacco to chiropractic treatments for back pain. He died of throat and tongue cancer at age seventy-nine in 2002.

The federal court could not reach a verdict regarding Edgar Ray Killen, so he went free in 1967, but in 2005, the state of Mississippi finally did the right thing and charged him with manslaughter. The former Klansman and Baptist minister was then found guilty. Killen had bragged about the murders. His conviction by Neshoba County jurors on June 21 was handed down exactly forty-one years—to the day—after the 1964 murders. Outside the courthouse, people cheered, and some cried. Sentenced to sixty years, he died in the Mississippi State Penitentiary at age ninety-two in 2018.

The movie *Mississippi Burning* depicted the FBI's search for the murderers of the three civil right workers during that awful summer of 1964. When I went to see it, I sat in the dark for two hours remembering Mother and me on that summer day in the sweltering packed courthouse. Whenever the case is written about, I think, *We were there. We looked the killers in the face.*

One winter day in London, where I was staying at Ennismore Gardens with my friend Victor, I set off for the Old Bailey. The guards always remembered me even if a year or two had passed since my last visit, and on this afternoon they advised that the best trial, a murder, was in courtroom number seven. A guard carefully eased open the door, and I went in to join the spectators in the gallery. I saw only one empty place and made my way toward it as several people looked up and stared at me. There were whispers as I settled myself. It's not a tremendous gallery and is above the courtroom; sitting in it, one looks down at the action below.

The trial was in full swing. I had no idea who had been murdered or who the defendant was. All I understood initially was that a Canadian woman had been unfaithful. A portrait was painted of her as a selfish, callous, self-centered woman who had no respect for her adoring husband and little regard for her young children. She'd become involved with an Englishman who was working in Toronto, and when she told her husband of the affair, he was desolate.

On the stand, he was a sympathetic figure. Handsome, with a Canadian accent, he wept as he spoke about how much he loved her. He had begged her to break off the affair, but she wouldn't. This went on for months. He lost weight, couldn't sleep. Desperate, the husband impetuously flew to London and went from Heathrow directly to the hotel of his wife's lover. His idea, he said, was to ask him to leave his wife alone. The husband forgave her, he still loved her, and he wanted her back as the mother of his children.

In a voice choked with emotion, the husband described how he'd gone to the hotel room and confronted his rival. The man had mocked him. Usually a calm man, the husband carried a small pen knife, as it was his habit to sharpen his pencils with it. He drew the knife and stabbed the laughing Englishman, who died before help could arrive.

Of course, we spectators were breathless. It was horrifying; it was sad. This mild-mannered, even-tempered Canadian had been driven to a crime of passion by a heartless, cheating femme fatale. Drained, his testimony finished, he was helped from the witness box.

The bewigged judge banged his gavel, and court adjourned for the day. The other spectators and I stood and began to file out. People were talking behind their hands and giving me very harsh looks. I couldn't understand it. Was I being paranoid? I'd entered silently, minded my manners, and now was filing out with everyone else, and yet people were staring at me.

I went back to Victor's apartment at Ennismore Gardens, and as we cooked dinner I told him all about the trial. "Victor, I don't know why, but people were looking at me, and when I went out into the street there was a small crowd, and I thought people were saying, 'There she is!' It was kind of awful. One woman said, 'Bold as brass!' as I walked toward the tube." I took a sip of wine. "I really felt she was talking to me!"

Meanwhile Victor had been rummaging in the living room wastebasket for something. He came into the kitchen with the previous day's *Daily Mail* and, thumbing through it, demanded, "Were you wearing your tan coat?" I nodded, and he spread the paper open on the table. "Look!"

The wife had been spotted in London some days before and a photographer had snapped her picture. She was tall; wore my double-breasted, camel-hair coat; and had dark, shoulder-length hair like mine; the image was so like me that I recoiled in shock.

I don't know what happened to the Canadian husband or to the unfaithful wife because I flew to Rome the following day.

My first murder. A wealthy widow named Irene Silverman disappeared from her beaux arts mansion on the Upper East Side on the Sunday after the Fourth of July 1998. I was living in the Crow's Nest a few blocks away on Sixty-Fifth and Lexington at the time, whereas Mrs. Silverman's house was between Park and Madison on a swankier bit of real estate.

Accused of murdering Mrs. Silverman were a mother and son from Las Vegas, Sante and Kenny Kimes. The tabloids called them Mommy and Clyde, and labeled them grifters and con artists, which they were.

I'd worked for two years, with four lawyers and several other P.I.s who had always gotten fired, in preparation for the trial, which lasted ten weeks. Day after day we'd been in the courtroom hearing hours and hours of testimony and now, in May 2000, it was over: Sante and Kenny Kimes were convicted in a case with no body, no weapon, no witness, no confession, and no forensic evidence. I'd gotten to know the pair of them as well as anyone, maybe better than anyone, and I was sure that Sante had killed people—*other* people—and gotten away with it. But I'd soldiered on doing my best, chasing obscure possible witnesses and trying to confirm dead-end alibis, hoping they hadn't killed Irene Silverman. I believed strongly that everyone deserves a fair trial, and I told myself that if there was evidence out there that would prove their innocence, then it was my duty to find it.

On this bright spring day in the courtroom, the word *guilty* rang out again and again and again—118 times, on all 118 counts.

I felt hollow inside. The numbers swam in my head. Part of me was relieved that they would never walk the streets again. I knew they were dangerous. I had spent hours with them at 100 Centre Street every week, discussing leads and possibilities. When Sante would call from behind her grate across the little lawyers' area to Kenny behind his grate, "Cici is the only one to understand our case! She is going to get us out of here, and we're going to take her for a big steak dinner!" I would shiver. Several dinner guests had never been seen again after a meal with the Kimeses.

The sentencing was the following month. Another day in the courtroom we had come to know so well. Judge Uviller described Sante as "a sociopath of unremitting malevolence" and Kenny as a "remorseless predator." The judge called Sante "the most degenerate defendant who has ever appeared in this courtroom" and sentenced her to 120 ⅔ years at Bedford Hills Correctional Facility, which is a short train ride from New York City.

Kenny was sentenced to 126 ⅔ years, to be served at the Clinton Correctional Facility in Dannemora, just thirty miles from the Canadian border.

The next time I saw Sante and Kenny was in a courtroom in Los Angeles, where they were being tried for the murder of David Kazdin. New York governor George Pataki had extradited them at the request of California governor Arnold Schwarzenegger. Sante had insisted to her California lawyers that I was the only person to understand the case because it was part of the Silverman case. "It's all *the same case*!" she would swear to me on the phone, over and over again. The L.A. lawyers, confused and exhausted by her demands, finally surrendered and flew me out to be the consultant to the defense team.

If convicted, Sante and Kenny would be the first mother and son to face the death penalty in U.S. history.

Kenny frightened me when I saw him take the stand. Gone was the tall, handsome, clean-cut college student I'd seen a few years earlier. I'd been struck in New York by his hands; his nails were always immaculate. How did he manage that, I wondered. Manicures at Rikers Island seemed unlikely. Now, in Los Angeles, he loomed as a dark force. His brown hair was long, slicked back in a ponytail, and he had a thick mustache. He wore an orange jumpsuit and handcuffs, which glittered in the light when he raised both hands to swear to tell the truth. It was June 2004, four years after the sentencing in New York, and he looked big, strong, and very menacing. I supposed prison had made him that way.

Kenny had finally turned against his mother. The lawyers in New York had waited in vain for it to happen, but now it had. Kenny had made a deal with the Los Angeles D.A. to tell the truth about both the Silverman and the Kazdin murders, and in exchange the death penalty would be off the table for both him and his mother.

So began his testimony of how he had pulled the diminutive eighty-two-year-old woman into her own bedroom as she struggled. His mother turned the TV on and then hit her in the head with the stun gun. Irene Silverman was only four feet ten inches tall. Kenny described his fingers around her throat as she fought. I thought of her dying, in her own bedroom, on a particularly bright and lovely Sunday afternoon in July as Manhattan pulsed with life outside. She struggled to breathe as I sat in the Crow's Nest a two-minute walk away, probably reading the Sunday papers.

Kenny killed her, killed her, killed her raced through my mind. I could hear my heart beat in my ears. All those hundreds of times, two years of staring into his face, into those clear, green eyes, and having him swear he was innocent, and I'd wanted to believe him. Yes, maybe he and his mother had killed *other people*, but not poor Mrs. Silverman.

Now Kenny's words hung in the air like subtitles between us. I was mesmerized.

Of course, the details of shooting David Kazdin were just as horrible. In the courtroom I could see the victim's daughter in silhouette, the tears shining on her face. But the moment I remember most vividly was from the Silverman murder, Kenny's voice saying, "I didn't know how long to squeeze. It seemed like a long time." I thought of his clean fingernails, his large hands, and how tiny Irene Silverman had been. I had wanted to believe him and I had believed him all this time and I'd been wrong. The earth shifted for me.

When Jamal Khashoggi, the journalist at the *Washington Post*, was murdered in Istanbul in 2018, I thought of the power of the Saudi royal family and recalled a day at the Old Bailey a few years earlier. The guards told me that the most interesting murder trial that day was in a closed courtroom. Absolutely no one allowed in. Of course, I was interested. "No, can't let you in," I was told by several guards. I hung around in the corridor, chatting to them. One guard somehow got the idea that I should be allowed in.

One enters in the top row of seats as if in a very small stadium, with the bewigged barristers, witnesses, judge, and defendant below. The entire spectator section was empty except for five Saudi men. I walked down the short aisle and brazenly sat in the front row a few seats away from them. A railing was in front of me, like the railing in the front row of the balcony of a theater. And a trial is theater. There was a rustle among the Saudi men and whispering; I suppose they were relatives of the defendant or representatives of the Saudi government. Heads turned on the floor of the courtroom—even the judge looked up—as I sat down. Later I learned that I had been mistaken for a Saudi family member. The proceedings were several hours of testimony and CTV footage that have haunted me ever since. The defendant was a Saudi prince in his twenties who had beaten a servant/companion day after day in one of London's best hotels and taken him to restaurants, night clubs, and all around the town as the young man was dying of head injuries. A tape of a vicious beating in a hotel elevator was shown again and again. The thin young victim made no attempt to defend himself and seemed too exhausted to do more than try to protect his face, cowering, as the punches landed.

The trial ended with a conviction, but the monster—who smirked and fidgeted in the dock during the ghastly testimony—was to be allowed to serve his sentence in his home country. Justice for a Saudi royal family member? Didn't happen in England.

I was on the subway platform in Astoria at quarter of five one morning but discovered that the trains don't start to run until half past. I paced as I waited. All the way there, I worried I'd be late, but I was in front of the federal courthouse in Brooklyn at six-fifteen, in plenty of time. My credentials from World Radio Paris had made me a member of the press and I shivered with them and everyone else in the cold predawn darkness for about an hour until the doors opened. The tightest security—all the guards wore bullet-proof vests, and large dogs strolled back and forth everywhere I looked. At nine-thirty we'd gone through our second set of metal detectors and put on our shoes again and were in the courtroom.

I had been warned it would be "grueling," but I thought a day with El Chapo was like *Breaking Bad* on steroids. Joaquín Archivaldo Guzmán Loera was the architect of an empire spanning the globe, his army of men moving tons of cocaine, heroin, and methamphetamine. Doing whatever was necessary to deliver. So much murder, so many millions.

El Chapo looked small and very ordinary without his signature mustache. He sat ten feet away from me with his defense team; I stared at him all day long, thinking of his power and of his headline-grabbing escapes from custody.

From my place in the first row I saw one of New York City's most famous criminal-defense lawyers in action: Jeffrey Lichtman. An El Chapo deputy was on the stand ratting out his former boss. Lichtman would ask a question, the translator would blah blah in Spanish, the witness would often say, "Si, Señor," the translator would turn to Lichtman and say, "Yes, sir," and Lichtman would ask the next question.

Once the witness's monologue was translated as "He came and my bodyguards could not kill him. They were not able. They were not professional."

Lichtman feigned amazement. "Your bodyguards were not professional? Where did you find them? On Craigslist?"

Things could get very adversarial. Three times the judge admonished, "Mr. Lichtman, you are shouting!"

I was sitting beside a *New York Post* journalist, a Venezuelan, and a writer for *New York* magazine, but there were journalists from all over. They said all that translating gave them plenty of time to take notes. I felt among friends, as Phoebe Eaton was there and she'd been my editor at *Talk* magazine when I had written about Sante and Kenny Kimes. Mother and daughter courtroom artists Shirley and Andrea Shepard were sitting two seats away from me, drawing in colored chalk on easels propped on their knees. I'd known them during those endless weeks of the Kimes trial in 2000.

During a break we all stood, some of us wandered out, though even going to the ladies' room meant emptying pockets, removing shoes and belts, and taking another trip through the metal detectors. The defense team was half a dozen people sitting at a long table a few feet from my front row so there was talk. The defense would attempt to sow doubt that Guzmán was the leader, to make him appear as only a cog in the wheel of this elaborate intercontinental distribution. It was trucks, boats, planes, tankers, tunnels, those human "mules," even submarines delivering product anywhere and everywhere, all the way to Kuala Lumpur. Tons of it. Every day. Every night. What does a ton of cocaine look like?

For me, the most meaningful sentence of the day came when one of the men on the stand explained why he finally decided to become a smuggler: "Hunger made me change my mind."

A few weeks later, on a very cold January day, I went to the trial again, and again, I was in the front row with other members of the press. The clock said nine-twenty-five and people were still standing, talking, taking off coats, getting settled in the courtroom. I was standing when the star arrived. El Chapo came in a side door with no handcuffs, no leg irons, again in a blue suit. Again, I noticed the absence of the mustache seen in all the photographs. He looked less vivid without it, diminished. It was like seeing a man who always wears glasses suddenly without them.

Guzmán arrived at the long table where the defense sat and turned toward me. His face lit up with a big smile, and he lifted his arm in a wave. I was horrified, thought, *My God, he thinks he knows me! Have I met him somewhere and don't remember? Miami? Santo Domingo? Costa Rica? Buenos Aires?* I sat down quickly and at that moment saw that a young woman with long black hair was in the row directly behind me. His wife!

Lichtman hurried in, deposited files on the defense team's table and then wiped his forehead and his upper lip with a tissue; his face gleamed with sweat. Emails from him to a lovely blonde client had been revealed online the evening before. They'd gone far beyond anything reasonable. They were embarrassing, sexual, even disgusting, and now Lichtman had to deal with his wife who'd known nothing of his affair until a reporter had called her for a comment. He patted his brow with Kleenex again and shook hands with his client. Guzmán motioned for him to wipe his upper lip and he did. So the top defense attorney was in deep trouble in his personal life and would probably be sanctioned professionally. Plus he was sweating. A lot.

I was in the last seat of the front row next to the wall and had to turn to the left all day to see the defense attorneys question the witness. Peripheral vision was not necessary. Guzman's wife was right there, at my left shoulder, a foot and a half of air separating us. Emma Coronel Aispuro was dressed in a black Lycra jumpsuit, she wore tan five-inch heels and a white vest which came to mid-thigh. Her hair was a beautiful, shining curtain of jet black, parted in the middle and falling absolutely straight to elbow-length. I noticed no jewelry, which surprised me. Later I was told security would not allow jewelry.

I'd heard she was American but had grown up in Mexico. At the age of eighteen, she'd just been crowned the Coffee and Guava Queen in her hometown pageant when Guzmán appeared with hundreds of security guards, saw her, and declared he was going to marry her. I did my math; today she was twenty-nine years old and he was sixty-one. They were the parents of six-year-old twin girls but El Chapo has another twelve children by other women.

A *narcotrafficante* who described himself as being in charge of heroin and cocaine going into Canada was on the witness stand all day. He'd begun his career at the age of ten, in Colombia, helping his brother and father dry the paste and package the coke. Now he was here in Brooklyn, wearing a prison jumpsuit, twenty feet away from his old capo, answering hundreds of questions posed by the Guzmán defense in an effort to show him as a liar. We all assumed that he was a liar, but the questioning went on and the stories came out. The Guzmán defense was trying to undermine his credibility with no success because, lying or not, the anecdotes were credible. Again and again he named Guzmán as his boss.

The witness told us about a woman in Canada who ran a modeling agency. Guzmán had wanted her to introduce models to officials visiting from Mexico City. Yes, she could do that. Then he wanted her to bribe a general with $10 million. If she was successful, she would be paid $1 million. Later she told Guzmán that the general had refused the bribe, and Guzmán was angry, didn't believe her, and ordered her killed. Our man on the stand was to find someone in Canada to kill her. He thought he might get the Hell's Angels to do it, but that didn't work out. Yes, she was still alive, he said.

This was the first time I'd heard of anyone in this trial refusing a bribe, so maybe she had lied. Later, in the afternoon, we would hear that a former president of Mexico had asked Guzmán for $250 million in return for suspending a nationwide manhunt; a compromise was reached, and the president was given a mere $100 million. According to the next day's papers, this revelation stirred little interest in Mexico, defining the country as rife with corruption, a place where bribery is common practice.

Kidnappings were described. *Retained* was the word used. Usually the victim owed Guzmán money and was *retained* until the money was found. Often, the victim was killed anyway.

We heard how a boat loaded with cocaine had been on its way to Ecuador when it had engine trouble off the coast of Costa Rica. To the rescue came the U.S. Coast Guard! Hurriedly all the cocaine was dumped overboard along with more than $1 million, which had been kept in an icebox. All into the deep blue Pacific.

Every person on board gave the U.S. Coast Guard a fake name. The Americans felt they should do background checks, but nineteen days later the searches were still fruitless. No record of any of them could be found, so the crew members were turned over to the Mexican Coast Guard. They were arrested at that point but were released after forty-eight hours. "How? Why?" asked the attorney. "Guzmán had us released. With a bribe."

Then the six of them all went to a house in Mexico that was equipped with security cameras that were monitored in the kitchen and the garage. The bathroom had a bathtub over a trap door, and a button behind the bathroom mirror. When the button was pushed the bathtub would open up "like the trunk of a car." Wooden steps led down to a tunnel that ended a mile away under a pool table.

It was easy to see Señora Guzmán at close range. I wanted to stare. She had beautiful dark eyes and a pretty-enough face that I thought was spoiled by thick, pouty, silicone-altered lips. Her fair complexion looked flawless from a distance, but I could see the heavy pancake makeup. I suspected that her breasts had been enhanced, but there was no doubt that her posterior has been augmented in a very grand way.

At the start of the proceedings she was sitting alone except for a courtroom artist eight feet away. She studied her perfectly manicured nails, which were painted a pale pink, until the first break, which was about two hours in. Her cuticles must have been fascinating. Her head was down, and that waterfall of glorious shining black hair fell forward as she concentrated on one hand, one finger at a time, and then the other hand, one finger at a time.

Later she was engrossed in carefully examining each hair for split ends. This labor took up the other hours of the trial, while a witness described Guzmán ordering this killing and that killing. She was absolutely mesmerized by the split-end situation, never looking up. Did she imagine that her husband, who killed so easily, might kill her? Or might give the order for her to be killed? Did she believe all she was hearing? Or was she tuning it out? Or was she hearing every terrible description, believing it, and only pretending not to hear it? Was she concerned about her husband, whom she would likely never spend a day or night with again? Was she relieved at the thought of a future without him? Maybe she was simply looking forward to being free of this tedious show of loyalty in this boring, drab courtroom. Maybe she was only looking forward to her next manicure.

A few of us in the press couldn't help but titter once in a while but there was never a reaction from behind me; she kept her focus. Guzmán's hit men were called The Anthrax Group. "*One* of his hit men groups," corrected a journalist at lunch. Our witness carried three guns on his person at all times. The translator parroted, "This is normal in Colombia."

Security was as tight as before with dogs outside the courtroom and the metal detector working overtime. The government was shut down because of a stalemate in Washington at the time. I asked a guard about it, and he told me they were being paid and would be paid until the money ran out. There was talk that the trial would stop and only start again when the shutdown ended. Everyone had heard rumors and everyone had ideas.

I worried about the security team on the eighth floor. Several of the U.S. marshals were so fat, with such enormous bloated torsos that their flak jackets looked like halter tops and left their vast bellies unprotected.

In mid-afternoon, a few journalists left for the press room to file stories. Next to me had sat a Venezuelan who wrote for the Spanish edition of the *Washington Post*; when she left a writer for the *New York Times* slipped into that space beside me.

Objections to Lichtman's questioning rang out again and again and were usually sustained by the judge. By half past four, we were all exhausted, El Chapo was led out surrounded by his security and his beauty-queen wife disappeared in a flash of black and white.

I watched the courtroom empty. I'd been ten feet away from the world-famous Mexican *narcotrafficante*, who has allegedly killed or ordered the murder of between two thousand and three thousand people—but my Mexican friend at the laundromat told me he killed entire families if someone declined to work for him or wanted out, so she imagines that is a low estimate. She also said he gave money to build schools and hospitals. Some Mexicans love him.

El Chapo is five feet five inches tall with a second-grade education, yet his worth is estimated at $4 billion. This drug lord, called the most dangerous man in the world, sat before me hour after hour, without his mustache, wearing a suit and a tie, looking quite small and, the defense hoped, innocent.

MY RECKLESS TWIN

Broadway. Bright lights. Theater marquees. More than five hundred years ago it was an Indian trail. Then it was named Brede weg by the Dutch. The Broadway I know is different from yours. Just west of it, the buildings are honeycombed with sweatshops manufacturing counterfeit goods. A few blocks away from *Hamilton* there are factories running twenty-four hours a day, manned by illegal immigrants who are sometimes locked in. When I see this, I wonder if they'd be able to escape in case of a fire. People assume all the fake handbags, designer clothes, watches, and T-shirts are coming in from other countries but they're not.

It was my turf about five days a week. I was always crossing it back and forth on my way to meet the bad guys and then zigging and zagging back to the office so no one could follow me. I would be wearing a hidden video camera. Assuming a name I picked out from my *What to Name the Baby* book, I'd adlib about my boutique in another state, having memorized possible addresses, probable phone numbers, and appropriate zip codes. I was Veronica or Charlotte or Valerie; the list was long.

It was a sunny day in April, and I was on Broadway at Thirty-Eighth Street, minding my own business, on my way back to Mickey's office on Thirty-Fourth Street, which was over a little drugstore between Madison and Park. Parker's had imploded in financial ruin and was no more. Mickey and I were on our own.

I was mentally hammering out the report I'd write. Asian male, early fifties, five foot seven, 160 pounds, scar on the left cheek. I was delighted when a Korean had an identifying scar. I could discern Korean from Vietnamese, and I could pick out Chinese easily but telling one Korean from another Korean I sometimes found worrying. I was thinking of the study that claimed that there was a forty percent higher chance of a mistake when identifying a subject of a different race. I agreed. So I was walking along, thinking about his scar. In the nineteenth century it could have been a dueling scar, but I doubted this Korean selling handbags had been fighting any duels.

"Stephanie! Stephanie!"

I didn't turn, didn't slow down. Suddenly right in front of me was a large man, saying, "Stephanie! Wait up!"

Middle Eastern, probably Lebanese, six foot one, 190 pounds went through my mind. "Sorry. You have the wrong person," I said, trying to move past him.

He sidestepped and blocked my way. "Stephanie! I recognize you!"

"I'm not Stephanie," I said. "You've made a mistake."

"Yes, yes you are! It's your voice, it's your face! I'm sure!"

Damn. Hell. I couldn't just break into a run. I'd have to keep denying until he gave up. I wondered what deal I'd made with him. I wondered if the Joint Terrorist Task Force had done a seizure with information I'd given them.

I shook my head. "No. Sorry. I'm in a bit of a hurry. Please."

He seemed to be taking up a lot of space in front of me, and he was so sure. And, of course, he was right to be sure.

"You were in my store last week. I know."

"I've never seen you before. I don't live in New York. You've made a mistake."

"No," he said. He still blocked my way. I am five foot nine barefooted, but I felt small.

"Oh!" I said. "I know what's happened!" I watched his face; he was rapt. "You met Stephanie!"

He nodded. "Yeah. That's you!"

"No," I shook my head. "That's my twin sister. Stephanie."

"You have a twin?"

"Identical." I stopped. "She must be in New York again."

"Whadda ya mean?"

"We haven't spoken in two years. She's . . . she's trouble. Listen, whatever she's up to . . ."

"Really?" he said. "She seemed perfectly nice."

"She's a wild card. Reckless."

He was staring at me, more intently than ever, seemed fascinated. "You look exactly alike."

I smiled. "I know. Not even our mother can tell us apart."

We chatted. I told him we'd had a fight over Stephanie's behavior but "I shouldn't go into that with you." I thought she was living in Atlanta now. "Be careful of her. Don't trust her."

He invited me to visit his store on Thirty-Ninth Street, and I said I would.

Of course, I already had his store, the contents, and him on video.

I wished him a nice weekend, and he grinned and wished me the same. He had a bright smile, warm brown eyes.

So it's all okay, I decided. My first boss had taught me to always finish the scam call with a good feeling. Don't make anyone second-guess the conversation or worry later that they've said too much. By phone or face-to-face, I tried to end every encounter with this in my mind.

I started walking downtown feeling lousy. Sometimes I liked the bad guys. And I knew that I had warned him to be careful—the opposite of what I was paid to do. And now, I had Stephanie, an identical twin, to worry about. I was retiring that name immediately and forever. It's a bit existential, I know, but crossing Broadway at Thirty-Fourth, I wondered who I really was.

ON THE ROAD WITH MOTHER

I called my work in Mississippi rural detectivery. I lived with Mother out at Turtle Creek one summer and got hired by Lyndon, who described himself as a former homicide detective with the Jackson Police Department. Mother was as excited as I was about my new profession and kept all my secrets, never once divulging anything to anybody. She would be eighty-four that September. We'd always been close but this summer there would be turning points. One specific one, for me anyway.

Mother and I gained pleasure and recognized beauty in the same things. It could be a crème-filled pastry or an orange sunset over the pine trees. We took swims at midnight, at noon, or just before the evening news with Tom Brokaw and a glass of wine. We had much the same sense of humor, and we never stopped talking.

Sometimes Lyndon would give me an assignment and an address a hundred miles away and I would take off in what Lyndon called the perfect surveillance vehicle: Mother's little white station wagon.

One afternoon in July, the phone in the kitchen rang and I leapt for it like a Doberman going for sirloin. "Sure. Yes, okay." I was writing frantically. "I'm just about to drive into town. After I pick up Mother at the dentist and drop her off back here then I can go."

I listened, glancing at the big kitchen clock. "I'll call you tomorrow."

I tied my sneakers, grabbed the car keys and my canvas bag with my wallet, a camera, and a notebook in it, slammed the front door, and in two minutes was in the car barreling toward the dam.

"Mother, Lyndon wants me to drive to this place called New August—no, New Augusta," I explained when I'd picked her up at Dr. Carter's. My watch said quarter of three. "I have to pick up a summons, actually get it issued at the courthouse, and then go and find this truck driver and talk to him. Get a statement."

"Fine." Mother was arranging her pocketbook between her ankles on the floor of the front seat.

"Do your seat belt," I said automatically because she nearly always forgot. "Now, I can drive you back to the house or . . ."—I thought aloud— "or you can come with me. Which do you want?"

"I'll go with you."

"Great. There's a map in the dashboard. You can be navigator. Just tell me north or south."

We were off. First stop was a filling station to find out exactly where the town was and then, in minutes, we were on the highway.

"We could take the Trace," said Mother.

I turned onto it as soon as I could, and we both raved about how green and beautiful it was. "Think of the Indians cutting this through the wilderness," said Mother.

"And the buffaloes wearing a path down before the Indians."

We both appreciated the history of these parts. I told her about my research for *Mississippi Diamonds*, a novel I wrote in Ottawa on the dining room table. "The bandits on the Trace would kill everyone so there'd be no witnesses, and this was good for me and for the story. It all takes place before the Civil War in the Mississippi Territory, in 1823. I put a lot of scenes in Natchez Under the Hill in a whorehouse . . ." Mother and I had been to Natchez several times, had lunch in a little place Under the Hill. The miles rolled by.

"This case is one of Lyndon's insurance things," I started to explain. The road stretched before us like a wide gray strip of chewing gum; on either side of the road were clouds of green woods. "A truck driver named Jake Hargrove was hauling logs from Pearl to Star, then down to Bay St. Louis and there was an accident and a man was killed."

"How awful," sighed Mother. Then she did what I knew she'd do. "Remember that couple—can't think who she was the daughter of—but anyway, I do remember they drove away on their honeymoon and—"

I hated this story. I'd heard it from Mother years ago and never forgotten it. I knew she had to tell it again and that I couldn't escape hearing it again.

"The logging truck ahead of them didn't have the logs tied down the right way, and one of them slipped and came right through the windshield of their car, and both of them, the bride and groom, were killed." She shook her head. "I remember hearing about it just the day after the wedding. Everybody was still talking about the reception."

"Awful," I broke in. It was such an old story that insurance, liability, and lawsuits didn't enter into it.

I thought that New Augusta was about a hundred miles away, just past Hattiesburg. Mother was saying that Dr. Carter was such a good dentist. "Did you know that he and his wife, Gail, were missionaries, all over the world, and that's how they met?"

The lush, green landscape met the clear, blue sky and we, in the perfect surveillance vehicle on the chewing-gum-gray road, proceeded through the middle of it, like a bug crawling across a painting.

We talked about Lyndon, and I think Mother liked him as much as I did. We talked about people in Jackson. Somehow Mother's friend Peggy Thompson came up, and Mother said, "She's dead now. Years ago. Killed by soap operas." I pictured a deranged character in *As the World Turns* leaping out of a black-and-white TV screen and giving poor Mrs. Thompson a heart attack. But no, that wasn't how it happened at all. "She just got addicted to them. She'd go upstairs to her bedroom after lunch and pull the curtains and be there in the dark for hours. Right up until Casper came home from the office."

"Mother, what does that have to do with—I mean—you can't die from watching soap operas."

"It was the bourbon, of course," Mother stated. "She had to have the bourbon to go along with all the stories. One after another, all afternoon, five days a week, one bottle after another. Casper Thompson used to play golf with your father. He had no idea."

Wasn't clear to me if Mr. Thompson had no idea or Daddy had no idea. I didn't want to pursue it.

We passed the sign to Star and agreed that I should live there someday because of my green star tattoo. "And because of your detective firm," said Mother. We'd named it Green Star Investigations only the week before. We passed a sign to Mendenhall, and Mother remembered a nice woman who had lived there and had something to do with the Sierra Club. A sign for Sanatorium whipped by, and then the sign for Magee. "Oh, they had terrible race trouble there," said Mother. Mount Olive was the next little town. "I always think it sounds like Lebanon and not Mississippi," I said. Mother wondered aloud if they grew olives there. "I don't know," I answered. "The climate might be okay for them, come to think of it."

The car sped along with the two of us chattering away. I guess it was at some point around Collins that we made a mistake, and before I knew it, we were off in the unknown, and I was trying my damnedest to get on the right stretch of highway. We got lost, and we had to drive so many miles in order to turn around that when I glanced at my watch I was shocked at how late it was. Nobody else was on the road, so I said, "Mother, I'm gonna speed up. You've got your seat belt on so don't worry."

Mother nodded. "Fine."

I pushed the little car up to eighty-five and we really moved. Mother was unblinking, completely composed beside me. There was no bracing against a door handle or the glove compartment, no nervous hand-clenching in her lap. Absolutely blasé.

"Dammit!" I said. "We are miles away, and Lyndon told me the courthouse closed at five!"

Mother looked at her watch. Four-forty-seven. "You'll make it," she stated.

"I don't think so." I grimaced. We were still at least fifteen miles from New Augusta, and then, once I got there, we'd have to find the courthouse. "If we don't get there in time I think we'll have to find a motel and spend the night and start this all over again tomorrow morning."

Mother said quietly, facing straight ahead. "We'll make it."

I looked at my watch and then pushed the little station wagon up to ninety. Mother didn't say a word, but I felt the car protest with a little trembling, so I let the speedometer needle fall back to eighty. The perfect surveillance vehicle had probably never been driven this fast, and it was frightened.

It was exactly five o'clock when we turned into New Augusta. "So close!" I swore, and Mother said calmly, "Something will happen. You'll make it."

I wanted to go fifty in the little town but didn't dare. I yelled out the window at a little boy on a red bicycle, "Where's the courthouse?" and he pointed and said, "Thataway."

Then I floored it, going thataway. When I didn't see the courthouse in five blocks and there was nothing but tree-lined streets, I shouted out the window at a couple of old men sitting on a park bench, "Hey, where's the courthouse?" and they took off their straw hats, both of them, and then said, "Ya jes go down to the stop sign and turn left." I waited and the one with glasses said, "Go on straight aftuh that and you cain't miss it."

Mother called, "Thank you" out the window as I floored it again. There it was. Big building, big steps, couldn't miss it. The Perry County Courthouse. My watch said four minutes past five.

"Mother, I'll leave the keys for you! Wish me luck!" I jammed the shift into Park and heard her say, "Something will happen."

I ran up the steps three at a time and pushed open the double glass doors, which had the hours plainly printed on them. Not locked, good sign. I ran down the darkened hallway with the shining linoleum floor looking for any door that said "Circuit Court," and when I found it I burst in. A woman sat at a desk, behind a waist-high counter, going through her pocketbook as if looking for a lipstick. "Oh! Thank goodness, you're still here!" I cried. "I've come all the way from Jackson and have to get a summons issued!"

"Well, now, the clerk's gone fer the day. Jes left," she said. She was lethargic, lackadaisical, entirely unconcerned. "You jes missed him." She looked at her watch and I looked at mine. "He's prob'ly on his way ta his sistuh's house fer supper, unless he's goin' home first ta check on his dawg."

It was five-oh-seven.

"Isn't there anyone else who could take care of this for me? I've driven a hundred miles." I sighed.

She looked at me. I guess I looked pretty desperate. Then she said slowly, "Well, he does have a car phone. Lemme see if I kin git him on that. I jes might have the number here."

I couldn't believe it. The clerk of the Perry County Circuit Court turned around in his car, and came back to the courthouse for me and issued the summons, and in fifteen minutes I was getting into the front seat telling Mother all about it.

"I knew something would happen," she said, smiling.

I laughed with relief.

I pulled out Lyndon's directions to Jake Hargrove's place. They seemed pretty basic. "We're supposed to go out of town heading east then south for four miles and then get off the highway and pass under two cement bridges," I said.

I checked the odometer and off we went. In ten minutes we'd gone under one cement bridge but not a second. "It says after the two bridges . . ." I grabbed my notes from the dashboard. "Why can't we find that second bridge?"

We decided to skip the second bridge. The thing was—there was no one to ask. We seemed to be deep in Perry County, at least I hoped we were, but no nearer to a certain fruit market which stood at the turnoff.

"Look, there's a watermelon stand!" called out Mother and I slowed the car.

"Must be it. They're selling peaches, too. Must qualify as a fruit market. That must be what he was talking about." We turned off, went down the dirt road past the fruit stand. There were only three mailboxes and none of them said Hargrove. Then we went another mile down the dirt road, and I saw a house back in the pine trees. "I'll get out and ask them if they know him or where he lives. This is crazy."

I parked in the driveway of the little house, which I realized was actually a trailer planted deep in the trees. Whitewashed tires circled it and covered the darkness between the ground and the trailer itself; they looked like milk-soaked Cheerios. There was a truck parked on the other side of the driveway in the grass. Dogs barked as I read the door: HARGROVE TRUCKING, DANCING DEER, MISSISSIPPI.

The door of the trailer opened, and a fat, pink-faced woman called to me. "We bin waitin' on ya!"

I ran back to the car and got pen and paper. Mother said she was fine, and I left her the keys so she could play the radio if she wanted. Hound dogs wailed mournfully in the woods beyond. Then I sprinted back to the open door and took the little steps up as if boarding a ship.

The air conditioner was on high and blasted me in the face when I entered the living room. It smelled like chemicals and was icy cold. My bare arms were covered with goose bumps as I reached out to shake hands with Jake Hargrove. He was a large man in a brown cotton plaid sport shirt and overalls; he had big ears and false teeth and a face as wrinkled and tan as an old wallet. I don't know why but I immediately felt sorry for him. From the looks of him, Jake had been an athlete at one point in his life and, if asked, would probably say, *"Yeah, I played ball in high school."* Now, in his early sixties, he had that shrunken, stringy neck some football players get, and a bit of a turkey wattle showed above the white T-shirt. I explained about the summons and the statement and told him how I had to ask, not about the accident, but about who'd paid him for transporting the logs.

"That was Jimmy. Jimmy Hill. He loaded my truck up when he

realized he couldn't take all them logs on his. He worked for another company called Turner's."

"This very well may affect who has to pay the insurance out," I explained.

He talked and I wrote down what he said and I asked him for dates and he told me. I resisted the impulse to rub my bare arms and scream that I was freezing. Then I read everything back, and he nodded, and I handed the yellow legal pad over to him, and he read it and signed. I looked around the rectangular room. It was about eleven feet wide. There was a bright-yellow shag rug, duck decoys on a nearly empty bookshelf, and two paintings of those big-eyed children by Keene. A massive television was on with the sound off; images flickered in the bright primary colors of a cartoon. *Good Housekeeping, Popular Mechanics,* and *Field & Stream* lay on the coffee table. Beside the Naugahyde recliner was a little table with a half-empty mug of beer on it. I guessed having a solicitous wife meant you didn't drink out of the can. I could hear a sizzling noise behind me, and I smelled meat cooking.

The pen moved back and forth as he signed and dated the page. Then I heard a sniffling noise and realized it was Jake Hargrove. "I'm sorry," he said. "I never in all my life thought such a thing would happen." His eyes were bloodshot and filled with tears. He fumbled in his overalls for a handkerchief and then held it over his nose and blew. But the tears kept coming. He mopped his face roughly and tried to clear his throat to speak. "I kept meanin' ta git the rig fixed. I wuz driving as far as I could to thuh right—practically on the shoulder when it happened."

"Did you hit him head on?" I asked. "Did your brakes fail?"

"No! Weren't nuthin' like that!" He blew his nose. "The trailer swung out, over the center line, and hit him. It'd done that before, but I thought I had it under control by practically driving mah cab on the shoulder like 'at." The man was grief-stricken. "It swung up—it jes dog-trailed right out behind me jes as he came on up over this little hill, and so it swung right on into him. He didn't have a chance." He mopped his face again. "A wife, three liddle kids." He closed his eyes for a second. "I dream about the accident. Bin near a year and I keep on seein' it happen."

"Jake! You bout through? Yore supper's gittin' cold!" called the woman. I could see her in a galley kitchen through a miniature doorway.

Then she walked out and, untying her apron, apologized for not offering me iced tea before this.

"No, thank you, Mrs. Hargrove. My mother's in the car, and I think we'll just turn right around and start back home."

My little exchange with her had given him a minute to compose himself. Maybe he cried every day, or maybe this had been the first time he'd talked about it in a while. I shook hands with the big jug-eared man and felt so sorry for him. His wife walked me the few steps to the door and opened it. "He dudn't like ta drive no more," she whispered. "All this jest about done broke his heart."

It was getting dark, the hound dogs were wailing, maybe to be fed. I got in the car and turned on the lights. "I'm sorry I was so long."

"You weren't so long."

I looked at my watch and saw that it had been just under twenty minutes, but I felt as if I'd spent days in that trailer with that big man and his story. I started the car, and we reached the main road and started back to the highway. The sadness of Jake Hargrove. It sounded like the title of a play. His wife. His broken heart. I wanted to shake the gloom of that poor man away, but I couldn't. We drove on in silence.

Mother and I got past Hattiesburg at dusk. As the sun was setting in Petal we saw a little white church with a sign out front that said, I CANNOT CONTROL THE WIND BUT I CAN TRIM MY SAIL.

Awhile later we parked beside a diner, and in minutes had ordered two meat loaf plates with mashed potatoes and okra. The waitress brought a little red plastic basket of cornbread, wrapped in a white paper napkin, as if that would keep the heat in.

Mother and I talked about how I'd hated kindergarten. "Right from the beginning," I said.

I hadn't wanted to be there. I wanted to climb trees. I hated sitting in those little chairs, I hated the games, I hated the blocks. So I waited until the teacher gave us the cookies and sneaked out the door and walked home. I wanted to be with my dog, Silky. I wanted to be catching crawfish. Everyone was very upset that I would walk home, crossing the street by myself, so finally, Christine, my black nurse, very fat and always giggling, stopped putting bows in my hair and walking me there. I stayed home until I was six. "Remember Christine? That giggle?"

The food came. The waitress set down heavy china plates, steaming, in front of us and refilled our water glasses from a metal pitcher dripping with condensation.

"Always 'tee hee hee,'" said Mother. "We should have her out to the house. How she'd love to see you."

I nodded and started to eat. In the blink of an eye I could remember— no, I could *feel*— what it had been like to be little. Christine was so good to me, but there'd been other maids before her. Gertrude, horrifyingly skinny, with all the veins showing on her stick arms, who'd take me out into the garden at night and tell me stories about wolves. We'd rock back and forth on the glider under the trees in the dark, and I'd cower, bare feet tucked under me. Mother and Daddy would have gone to a party, and I knew I should have been in bed. I was relieved when Gertrude was let go. Her departure had nothing to do with wolves; she'd been caught stealing the silver, taking it home in pillowcases.

"Driving like this today, makes me think of driving out to Whitfield," said Mother. There had been one summer between my years at college, after the divorce—hers, not mine—that I'd lived with Mother at Turtle Creek and we'd done volunteer work at the state mental hospital near the little town of Whitfield. Everyone called the hospital itself Whitfield; it was part of the vernacular. The entire population of Mississippi fell into four categories: you were in Whitfield, you belonged there, you had just gotten out, or you were ready for it.

Mother and I had been surprised at the place. It wasn't a snake pit.

114

The underpaid staff appeared to be kind. "I couldn't get used to the shock treatments though," I said. "And I remember entering the lock-in wards and feeling absolutely hollow inside when the door was locked behind me." A sound I'd told myself to never forget and I had not forgotten.

Mother began to poke at her mashed potatoes. "Well, I never knew about that," she said. "I remember how open it was. Everybody walking around, sitting on those benches under the trees, and even going fishing!"

Some of the patients weren't mentally ill but were retarded or had had a farming accident that had left them handicapped or breathtakingly disfigured. Most of them had no visitors, received no mail. Not ever.

I looked out the window and could see cars going by on the dark road. White lights, then red tail lights. People at the counter were laughing, drinking coffee.

I took a bite of warm cornbread. Sorrow swept over me. It was like the shadow of a plane when I was lying on my back in the grass. Years ago. It wasn't the sadness of Jake Hargrove. The darkness was mine, and it was very old darkness. Sudden, uninvited, and surprising. *Now*, I thought. *I have to*. I hadn't planned it. If anything, I'd planned to never say it. But now, I had to know.

"Mother, do you remember sometimes you weren't home for lunch? At the Old Canton Road house?"

"Well, when you were little I had the Junior League meetings, and that was a lunch maybe once a month; sometimes there was something at the old Country Club. The doctors' wives. The Auxillary." She picked up her glass. "I never played bridge."

I was studying her face. She sipped the iced tea and then put the heavy frosted glass down.

"It was before the first grade." She looked up at me and I stared back. "Daddy used to come home sometimes and make me take a nap with him."

"Why, where was I?" She looked confused. "I don't remember that you ever took a nap with him."

I'd done it. The words hung above us and between us like black letters on white flags. "You weren't there."

We stared at each other. Her face was anguished. "He made you—he made you?"

"I remember wanting to cry but thinking it wouldn't do any good. I remember that he would say, 'Come upstairs and we'll take a nap,' and I would feel so sick, so scared." I stopped. Mother was in pain across from me. The waitress came and refilled our water glasses, then the glass of iced tea. Ice cubes made crashing noises in the big metal pitcher. The noise actually hurt my ears. "I was so little that I had to hold onto the banister with my left hand and I could barely reach it and my legs were so short I had to take every step—every one of the stairs with one foot and then the other coming up to it and then the next—each step with both feet and having to take a little rest."

"Where was I?" Mother nearly moaned.

"It was when you didn't come home for lunch. Before I was in the first grade because after that I had lunch at school."

Mother had one hand at her throat. "I remember . . . I remember now that sometimes the maid would say that Dr. McNair had come home for lunch that day, or she'd tell me the next day, and I wouldn't know anything about it. Otherwise I'd have told the maid to have a main meal, a hot lunch for him. I'd . . ." Her face was white. "I'd be surprised. He would never mention it to me." She paused. "So it makes sense. This is when—" She couldn't finish the sentence.

I looked down at the meat loaf. "It's okay. It's over," I said. "I don't think I'm ruined or mentally ill." I almost made a joke about Whitfield. I felt tears come up in an odd place—like a swelling in front of my ears. I didn't want to cry here in this diner outside Hattiesburg.

"But he—" Mother was outraged, angry, not knowing what to say.

"I remember how afraid I was. Having to go up the stairs with him and he'd always close the bedroom door. Later I'd sneak away without waking him. Holding my breath. I'd be so terrified that he'd wake up when I turned the bedroom door handle. I had to reach up. It wasn't easy to turn it." I could feel the cold metal in my little hand. I could see the large room with the pale-blue-and-white striped wallpaper. The bedspread. *Dammit.* I could be so little again with so little effort. It was only one blink away.

This was the rare time Mother didn't blame herself. She could apologize for the rain, though she was more likely to proclaim it was "a restful day." I was glad she didn't blame herself. It was not her fault that it happened unless it was her fault for ever marrying him. Unless it was her fault for pretending nothing was ever really wrong enough to leave.

I blathered on, feeling as if a gate had opened and I were walking through it. "One of my friends once told me I could get hypnotized and recover what I'd written in all my lost journals from Africa. That I would remember every detail." I stopped. "Can't do that. Don't ever want to be hypnotized."

Two of my best friends knew. One told me she had suspected it long before I told her. "Mother, somehow I didn't know, not really know, until I was writing the novel in Rome. When I started it, I knew I had to write about something I knew. Everyone says that. So I stood on the terrace for ages trying to remember Mississippi, the heat, the slamming of a screen door and trying to fathom a way to get it across to somebody else using a piece of paper. In the beginning, I did this for hours every day. Just staring off at the sky and the green leaves of the trees over the Tiber. Floods of memories came back. Suddenly I knew what had happened. I could feel how long it took to get up the stairs. I could see the way the light came in the upstairs hall windows. I could hear the sound the door made when he closed it. Incredible details like being in an accident, everything in slow motion."

"How horrible. How disgusting."

"Yes, he was, wasn't he?" I said wondering if there was a hell.

Mother said, "It makes sense then. The lunches. The maid telling me he'd come home in the middle of the day. Of course, he knew when I wouldn't be there. It makes sense."

She had to absorb it logistically. The time, the place, the opportunity.

Mother wasn't one to fathom anyone's spirit. Her mind didn't work that way. She would fiercely resist plunging beneath the surface of a fact.

"You know what, Mother? I used to think he hated me because I looked like you but now I wonder if he hated me because he was afraid I might tell. Maybe..." I tried to laugh but made a gasping noise instead. "What if all those years of growing up and being bullied and called stupid every night at dinner and being afraid of him ... what if during all that time I had the power over *him*?" I stopped. "It would have been the only thing to ruin him. The great eye surgeon. The hero. The only thing no one could have accepted. The only thing he couldn't have gotten away with."

The waitress took our plates, and we ordered dessert. I had pecan pie, and Mother had hot apple pie with vanilla ice cream on top and a slice of that orange rat cheese on the side.

We headed back toward Turtle Creek in the blackest of nights. I told her about Jake Hargrove and his wife and the trailer, and I described his great sadness. We talked about the sign in front of the church in Petal. I wanted Mother to print the phrase in her exquisite calligraphy and to frame it. "It's perfect, Mother. 'I can't control the wind but I can trim my sail.' Perfect."

We drove the last miles in silence. I had thought of my father thousands of times since his death but I never thought of those naps. I forgot them.

There had not been one word of praise or kindness from him, not one affectionate gesture in the eighteen years we'd lived in the same house. When I was little and we were alone together, he'd tell me he hated me and that he'd get rid of me, so I avoided him. But those dinners of taunts and tears I could not avoid. At the time, I never told anyone what he had done or what he had said to me.

I signaled and changed lanes to pass a truck on the highway and thought of Jake Hargrove. Tortured with remembering.

It was midnight when we crossed the dam into Rankin County. Minutes later, we pulled into the driveway. *Thank you, God, if you are up there in the clouds or in the pine trees or in the Pearl River. Thank you that she didn't know.* If she had known and not stopped him... if she'd suspected and let it happen, would I ever have been able to get over that? I had hated thinking she might have known but not had the strength to stop him. *That* is what I had feared and that was what I would now never have to accept. It was clear from her reaction that she had not known.

Or had she? She was so good at compartmentalization that she might have put the ugly truth aside so deftly and so long ago that she was genuinely surprised when I told her in the diner.

No. I pushed that possibility out of my mind. I must always remember her reaction. I'd told her because I had to look at her face. She hadn't known.

Of course, she hadn't.

I put the perfect surveillance vehicle in Park' as Mother unsnapped her seat belt. "That meatloaf! What flavor!" she said. "And the best apple pie I've ever had in all my life."

119

A BLACK EYE, A WHITE LIE

"Okay, okay, but you don't understand that Paris isn't New York. No one is going to see me if I just show up. Especially somebody like Monsieur Atti. I have to have—"

I was drowned out by my handler's orders. "Just get on the plane! It's in three hours. Your ticket's at the Air France desk."

"Okay," I sighed. "But who am I? Who do you want me to be?"

"You'll think of something." Dial tone.

So I was in a hurry. Within half an hour I was in a cab, my carry-on beside me on the seat. Traffic was bad, but I'd be checking in on time. We pulled up to the terminal and I got out, pulled my bag out, and put it on the sidewalk. I handed a few twenties in the driver's side, waited impatiently for the machine to spit out my receipt. I took it and the change and then leaned toward him to give him the tip just as I slammed my door. The metal corner of it hit me in the right eye with such pain my knees buckled. *I have no time for this*, I thought, with my palm pressing against my face. Not too much blood.

At check-in, the young French woman took my passport, handed me a Kleenex, then my boarding pass, and said, "Ask the flight attendant for ice." Threading my way down the aisle and finding my seat, a few people looked at me with interest. I held ice against my face until Newfoundland when it melted and became a dripping mess. My eye socket seemed to have a life of its own, a pulse, maybe even a heartbeat.

Near the end of the flight I looked in the little bathroom mirror and cursed. An orchid of deep purple, lavender, and fiery red had materialized. My right eye was still open which I took as a good sign.

At the hotel, the desk clerk saw me from the left, and when I turned to face him head on, gave a small gasp. I went up to my room and showered and put on my best jacket, wool trousers, and gold earrings and told myself I looked fine if you ignored my face. My wound with powder on it looked worse, so I decided to brazen it out.

A cab, the ritzy address, the sleek building. Elevator up to the executive offices of Atti's banking empire. Two women got on at the third floor, looked at me, then quickly averted their eyes.

I took a deep breath, exited the elevator, and walked toward the large polished steel dais manned by three seated receptionists. The guard dogs of the corporation. *My God*, I thought, *is every single person beyond elegant?* They were sleek and glamourous with bright red lipstick and perfect skin and, of course, were speaking French to me while I admired them. I answered, like a school girl, "Bonjour. Je suis désolée mais je ne parle pas français." They were all looking up, openly staring at my face. In awe. "I have just arrived from New York and am here to see Monsieur Atti."

"Oui! Yes, of course!" they chirped in unison. Then, as one, the trio looked down at their three large and identical appointment books and with manicured fingers traced the lines denoting the hours. Then they began to chirp with each other in what sounded like panic.

I was asked to please sit down and waved toward a reception area. I heard, "Non!" several times and the blonde said it was not possible. "Ce n'est pas possible!"

One of the greyhounds materialized in front of me and said she was very sorry for making me wait. "We apologize for the confusion for Monsieur Atti is 'aving lunch at thees moment, but would like you to join him? I 'ave written the address 'ere for you. It ees not far. A porter downstairs weel find you a taxi. Again, we are so sorry for the inconvenience to you."

The woman walked me to the elevator, looking quite worried. Moments later in the cab, I started laughing. I wondered if they thought their *grand fromage* had something to do with my eye. Then I stopped and thought, *What am I going to say to this Monsieur Atti? That certain people think he is laundering huge sums of money and I'm here to ask him about it?* I hatched a plan as the Peugeot purred through Paris. The lie was who I was and why I wanted to see him. A big lie or a little lie? Depended on how you looked at it. Make it a white one, I thought. Maybe crème-colored at the worst. Detectives don't talk about lies; we say "professional prevarication."

It was nearly eight o'clock in the morning in New York but here it was a sunny afternoon. The trees were just beginning to show green leaves, and Paris seemed radiant with the promise of spring.

The maître d' actually winced when I presented myself. "Of course, Madame, 'e ees waiting for you. Follow me."

The Monsieur Atti I'd known only from documents, only from his typed name, stood to greet me as did the three other men at the table. All suited and tied and prosperous-looking. Suddenly a chair was brought, I was seated, and the conversation became English. I thought my eye was the elephant in the room, the giraffe at the table, but, of course, nothing was said about it. I'd arrived at the end of the meal and, after a few moments of polite chatter about the weather in New York and had I had a good flight, the three men excused themselves and said goodbye. The table was cleared of all the wine glasses, plates, and utensils as Monsieur Atti openly stared at me. He was smiling, fair-skinned, Middle Eastern. His silk tie was lovely, as was his perfectly tailored suit. A shot of cuffs showed from each sleeve; the pocket handkerchief, the haircut, all conveyed elegance. His eyes were merry.

Monsieur Atti offered me lunch and kept smiling as if deeply amused by something. I said no thank you to lunch, as he had obviously finished, but we agreed that we would have dessert. He nodded and a waiter appeared instantly. Champagne arrived and was poured. It looked like liquid gold in the sunlight, which streamed in the window. Chocolate mousse appeared before me.

I honestly cannot remember what I told him. I can't remember who I said I was, but we got along. We got along so well he invited me to dinner that evening.

I had lunch with him again, dinners with him again. My handler in New York was ecstatic, and I assumed the high-powered lawyer receiving all this intelligence was very pleased, too.

During one call my handler told me if I went to bed with the subject, he would pay me a bonus. I held the phone away at arm's length and scowled before responding. "No nudity necessary. He will tell me what we need." *At dinner*, I thought, *not in bed*.

He took me to the best restaurants of Paris. The wine was divine; the food was five-star heaven. Monsieur Atti became Abdul. Conversation was about everything, but I'd always steer it to finance at some point. I'd lived in Geneva, I'd lived in Rome. We'd both lived in London, in Knightsbridge. He was well educated and sophisticated. I think he was married; he did have children, and he collected peridot. My second-favorite stone. Right after emeralds.

During one dinner, he made a nice toast. We sipped. He put the goblet down and laughed. "I must tell you that you amuse me so much."

I asked why.

"Because the first time you arrived, you came to my office and announced that you wanted to see me, and everyone became nearly hysterical because there was no appointment in any of the books. I am scheduled weeks in advance. You were so confident that all three of them were sure they had made a mistake and not written it down."

I laughed. "And I was so nervous because I don't speak French, and they were all so chic and Parisian. I was only pretending to be confident!"

I returned to New York feeling good about the trip because not only did I have information but the door was open for more intelligence-gathering. I went to my handler's office, and his secretary said, "My God!"

and then my handler saw me and said, "Christ! What the hell happened to you? Five rounds with Holyfield?" I shrugged. "Is it noticeable? It's really looking better." I paused. "No one in Paris ever mentioned it."

Abdul came to New York that summer, and we met for drinks and another lovely dinner. I had questions about a bank he dealt with and how certain transactions worked. As usual, the champagne flutes seemed always filled, and the wine flowed freely. I retreated to the ladies room, not once but twice, to slap my cheeks and take notes. It was infuriating to be having a good time, to like him, and to not be able to concentrate. I fluffed my hair, took a deep breath, and sailed back into the dining room.

Abdul was talking, was always telling me how this and that worked, and I would ask, "But why do that?" and he might say, "Because the tax code of France means that it would be unwise to not move the funds." On and on. Tonight he said, "I have the documents in my hotel room." I smiled and made a counter-offer. "Maybe you can tell me about those documents right here?" He didn't say anything. I added, "I think it might be dangerous to go to your hotel room."

Abdul Atti was a very urbane, highly intelligent man. I wonder if he knew who I really was, though I had no presence on the internet at that point. I wonder if he knew and fed me misinformation between sips of wine. I wonder if he knew and just liked my company and told me nothing of any importance, treating our meetings as simply a game. Whatever the truth of the matter, we did enjoy each other, and he obviously forgave me for lying to him.

The case led me to banks in Costa Rica, Miami, and New York, as well as Paris. I don't know the outcome, but I assume Abdul Atti was well insulated from arrest or prosecution. It was up to the lawyers in New York to pinpoint any criminality. No matter what, I liked him, but we lost touch.

On the afternoon of September 11th, 2001, I made my way up the stairs to the Crow's Nest and answered the ringing phone. My first call since the World Trade Center attacks a few hours before. The voice came from Paris. "I wanted to be sure that you were safe."

THE PASSION OF MR. YU

It was June, and Manhattan was surrendering to the sweaty embrace of summer. Today one of my sandal heels was sucked into the very asphalt when I crossed Madison, and I looked back with annoyance at the soggy tar. My childhood in Mississippi had been training for this—for nearly anything. I could handle hellish heat while strong men around me whined and wilted.

Mickey and I were now working several cases at a time together as Parker's was no more. In the final months, there'd been rampant paranoia. The idea that the office was bugged and our garbage was being stolen meant we'd bolt out of the warehouse and have conversations in the street among the hookers, who stood around nearly naked, looking bored.

At Parker's, everyone had respected Mickey, even the ex-cops who had more experience than he did. He had strong, even features, was handsome. He chain-smoked and couldn't stop. He'd tried the patch, and I wondered what he'd try next. He had quit drinking, and I thought maybe that was the most one could expect. Mickey was direct, tough, and sarcastic, but I knew that he kept a puppy picture of his dog in his wallet.

Now his office was a rented room over a drugstore on Thirty-Fourth Street. There was a window—"in case of fire," Mickey said—which was always open, despite the belching crosstown buses and the angry honk of horns.

It was a very small room, but only the week before, Mickey had expanded by renting the just-as-small room next door. We had to go out into the hall to go back and forth between the two rooms until Mickey took an axe and chopped a door in the wall between them. You had to remember to turn sideways a little and to step over a bit of remaining wall, since he didn't chop all the way down to the floor, but otherwise the opening was very convenient.

This was to be the summer Vinny the Chin Gigante would finally go to trial. Mickey had grown up with him in Greenwich Village and regarded him as a sort of uncle. I learned to never refer to him as The Chin but instead to quickly, lightly brush my hand under my chin. We followed the proceedings, read the tabloids aloud, always cheering on The Chin. This was also to be the summer we observed the passion of Mr. Yu as it unfolded from Hong Kong, across the Pacific, all the way to the Upper East Side.

Most of the time Mickey and I were enmeshed in an activity that is like running to a forest fire with a glass of water, chasing counterfeiters. We roamed Broadway, made forays into factories in Queens, and raced through the Holland Tunnel into Jersey. I would slink around Chinatown, wear hidden cameras and hidden tape recorders, and Mickey would videotape during car chases. I would fish names out of my *What to Name the Baby* book, and once in a while I'd order a new set of cheap business cards. Then I got so confident that I'd skip that and just brazenly face the bad guys, give them my new name, and tell them that I was having new cards printed because I'd changed our phone number. Then I'd rattle off the phone number, the fax number, and the address of my nonexistent boutique. Everybody always believed me, and not having the cards printed saved time. So Mickey and I were doing our bit for our clients, who were all the high-end designers, such as Chanel, Fendi, and Donna Karan, plus Walt Disney, Levis, the major sports teams, Nike, and dozens of others. But the counterfeiters just kept on getting more sophisticated, and the goods kept getting more like the real thing.

Mickey sometimes sensed I needed a change, so he'd take on a new case and give it to me like a birthday present. So on this baking-hot summer morning, there we were, sitting in the masculine splendor of a midtown Manhattan law office. Leather and chrome furniture, hunting prints on the wall, the cool breath of air conditioning. One of Mickey's four pagers had just spelled out that Gianni Versace had been murdered in Miami. Mickey was worried that he was wearing jeans and running shoes instead of a suit and I was telling him he looked fine. "I've gotta do a warrant in Brooklyn this afternoon. I can't do a warrant wearing a suit," he said.

"These lawyers know you're a detective. We don't spend all day behind a desk."

I was representing us, dressed for two as it were, in a navy-and-white silk dress and navy sling-backs with silver jewelry. Lawyers regard private investigators as an inferior species. Oh, yes. My philosophy is, Let them think it. Let them be seduced into complacency. But they'd better not dare be condescending to me. They'd better have good manners and pay my invoices. The dress was part of all this inter-professional sparring. I didn't ever want any lawyer to think I didn't know how to look okay.

Across from us on the other side of the coffee table was a lean Chinese man with a cell phone glued to his face. Six feet tall, very thin, in his late forties, wearing a white shirt, a skinny tie, and a lightweight summer suit. He kept closing his eyes behind black-framed glasses and then popping them open wide again during the conversation. His body twisted back and forth in the chair, animated, tense. Mickey raised his eyebrows nearly imperceptibly to tell me this was the client. I squinted in reply. *No. Ridiculous.*

The Chinese man was saying, "Mouw, mouw, mouw," again and again, louder and louder. Mickey was reading all his pagers, fishing them out of his briefcase one by one, and I was simply enjoying the air conditioning. "Mouw, mouw!" the Chinese was exclaiming.

Two lawyers appeared, in suits and bright silk ties. They introduced us to the man, Mr. Yu, and led us to a conference room. Mickey smiled one of his "I told you so, Charlie" smiles as we sat down at the boardroom table the size of a skating rink.

"Mr. Yu lives in Singapore, Kuala Lumpur, and Hong Kong, but much of his business is here in New York," began the Chinese lawyer named Dan Lo in American-accented English.

"Our firm," said the American lawyer, Bill Smithson, "handles a lot of Mr. Yu's affairs."

"I am here once a month," said Mr. Yu from his place of honor at the head of the table. "I have property here, business, always things. I take care of things." He nodded vehemently. "Things in New York."

We listened. It quickly became evident that one thing he took care of was named Lynn. But evidently somebody else was also taking care of her, and he was named Alvin.

Mr. Yu leaned forward with his long thin arms on the table and peered at me and Mickey through his glasses as if trying to decide how much we could be trusted to know. "You see this man, Alvin, work for me several years ago but then I fire him. I give him one hundred thousand to go away." He shook his head, upset. "Incompetence." He said the word very distinctly with disdain. Incompetence rewarded. Mr. Yu kept talking on and on. Some of what he said merited note-taking, most didn't. "Must know if Alvin married to her."

"Mr. Yu, may I ask a question?" I dared to break in.

Vigorous nodding, "Please, please."

"Do you want to know if they are legally married or if they are living together?"

"Good question!" he exulted, raising one index finger into the air over his bobbing head. "Want to know if live together. License not necessary. Where Alvin lives. I think she not tell truth about subletting apartment to endocrinologist. I think she use this apartment to meet Alvin, to sneak away from children, to hide from children. This man not good for children." He was agitated. "This man, other man, no good! I best for children! Many people say so. Other man I discover Japanese. Foreign. This man is American! Jewish! American! Not good for children!"

Dan Lo looked down at his papers. Mickey and I resisted the impulse to look at each other. Bill Smithson excused himself for another meeting. All this anti-American rhetoric hung in the air. *A third lover*, I thought. Alvin and Mr. Yu and now a Japanese. She's in bed with three nationalities. I remembered once dating a man who claimed to be working his way through the member countries of the U.N. I told him Mississippi had not joined.

"Claire like my daughter. She my goddaughter. Not my daughter but call me Daddy. I compute years. Cannot be but I regard as daughter." He passed photographs to us. One was of Lynn who "is forty-two but looks thirty" in jeans and sweater with two little girls in her arms. All three had straight black hair, Asian features, and sweet smiles. "Claire is eight years, little one five years."

"Adorable," I said. They were.

"Here more copies. Each have copies." He had about six sets of pictures, which went across the table to us, to Dan Lo. The men and I pored through our respective sets. One was a photocopy of Lynn's membership card at the Hong Kong Royal Jockey Club; another was a photocopy of her identity card. In one of the pictures she had a bouffant pageboy; in the other her hair was cut in layers. Her smile was shy in one and very confident in the other. More photographs of her with the kids. The identity card of a heavy-set Filipino who was the children's nanny. Wide, flat-faced with hair in a ponytail. A photo of the manservant, Jose, who lived with them. He looked rather sumo to me. I hoped I'd never have to meet him. I turned his photo facedown.

Mr. Yu was excitable. "Lucky I high energy," he said laughing at one point. "This take high energy." Sometimes Dan Lo tried to pull him back to the original thought or would dare to paraphrase in an effort to help me and Mickey. Half the time Mr. Yu would nod and say, "Right! Right!" in little dogmatic barks, and the rest of the time he would disagree with great animation and Dan Lo would retreat sheepishly.

"I know her for five years. She have many problems with banks in

Hong Kong. She go bankrupt. I help her. I give her five million dollars—a check—to help with problems. Later I find she not give money to the banks. She still in trouble with the banks. She spend money on something else."

Just when I expected Mickey to dive in with an offer of property searches, etcetera, to find where her money was, Mr. Yu suddenly raised his arms over his head and started shouting. "Money not important! Only money! I not care about the money!"

The room reverberated with his passionate outburst. Mickey said in an even voice, "Mr. Yu, I want to know exactly what you want us to do."

"She comes, she goes, you follow."

"But this round-the-clock surveillance can be a waste of time and"— Mickey paused—"money. I would rather set up a—"

But Mr. Yu was adamant. Every time she left the building we were to watch and report. "I want to know if Alvin drives the car. It my car. There!" He shuffled through the papers in front of him. "Registration papers. To my company in Ohio. License plate say 'Claire 2.'"

The car was a black Range Rover. Not exactly rare. He told us that Lynn had a house she rented in Connecticut. "I not allowed to go there. She go last weekend. Take children. Nanny, too. She drive Claire 2." He sighs. "Don't know if he goes. Not know. I called many times and she always answer phone. She say alone with children. Not know."

Lynn and Alvin are usually referred to as "he" and "she." He and she go out to dinner but not to lunch. "He have townhouse nearby. I have address but not good address." Mickey and I didn't look at each other. Lynn owned not one, not two, but three apartments in the luxury high-rise building on the Upper East Side. I knew the building. I suspected that Mickey knew every building in Manhattan and many in the outlying boroughs. He could tell you if it was doorman and practically describe the lobbies. I was delighted to know *this* building.

"Does she park the car underneath in the garage?" I asked.

"Yes."

"Does she pull out on Seventy-Second Street or on Second Avenue?" I persisted.

"Both. She use both exit."

She'd had five cars in four years. All presents from Mr. Yu. Then there was the matter of the limousine service she used, and her addiction to taxis. This little lotus blossom's feet never touched a sidewalk. There was Alvin's car but we had no plate. We could get it. He used to have a dark-blue Maserati. There were cell phones she used, had used, had changed the numbers on, and answered in different voices. Ten in all. She liked carrying several with her which maybe explained her not walking anywhere.

Mr. Yu poured through his papers, frantically looking for numbers. "Ah, here is one she have for while. This phone paid by family of dead husband." So Lynn was a widow. A merry one, if you believed Mr. Yu. And that family still paid her phone bills? Quite a trick. "Here. Write number." Mickey and I scrawled down number after number. "I hear there is photograph—wedding photograph—of her and Alvin on piano. Want you to get for me." Mickey and I were silent. We didn't do burglary. "It show they married. I want photograph."

Mickey said, "She has a cleaning woman?"

"Yes. Same Filipino for years. Travel with her."

Wow, I think. Never had I heard of anyone arriving anywhere with their own cleaning woman.

Mickey said he'd research marriage licenses. "That's better than the photograph." I was thinking marriage records were closed in New York State but maybe Mickey had ways I didn't know about.

Mr. Yu was not satisfied. "I want the photograph!" he insisted. Suddenly Mr. Yu's voice got very loud. "I want to know if she married! Married to a man who would send her—send his wife—to Hong Kong to sleep with another man for money!"

I love it. *This is a great case*, I think. Mickey and Dan Lo were silent. Mr. Yu's voice dropped to a whisper. "What kind of man," he said softly. He was in pain.

There were lots of details. Social security numbers. Dates of birth for the kids, for her, license plates, credit card numbers. Mr. Yu told us she would be leaving for Hong Kong in ten days. "This very busy time for her. She come to me the last week of month."

I tried not to think of the woman in the pictures and Mr. Yu naked in some red-and-gold, elaborately carved, Chinese opium bed, but, of course, I did think it. How much would he give her afterward? A check? Oh, yes. Or maybe a townhouse. Cash would be tacky. And bulky to carry.

Mickey was again making a last-ditch effort to pin down Mr. Yu about exactly what he wanted from us. Sounded like constant surveillance. Mr. Yu was nodding. "Yes, want to know her movements. Exactly. Everything she do. Every move she make."

I drew a little heart in the margin of my notebook and thought of "Every Breath You Take." Oh, Sting! When you wrote that, did you know Mr. Yu?

We were in the back booth of a diner on Second Avenue. Mickey ordered London broil, and I ordered a cheese-and-tomato sandwich. The waitress retreated. "I wanted to laugh so much that the tiny hairs on my arms were standing up," I said. "I was near exploding when he said he took 'slipping pill and slip and not know if she calls. You take, you out.'" I started to laugh. "You slip dip. Very very dip."

"Yeah, well you saw me when he passed me the other report and I saw Piggy's name! He hired Piggy three years ago to follow her! Piggy!" Mickey's voice was a wail of amazement.

"I know. I couldn't help but turn and look at you."

"Yeah, but Piggy did shit for him. And charged him thousands I bet! It was a shitty report."

We both knew what this meant. We'd been called in and the water had already been muddied. Piggy and who knows who else had done a lousy job, and the subject would be alert, nervous, watchful. It multiplied the difficulty of getting close, getting pictures, getting information. We were limping up to the starting gate with a sprained ankle. The client never wanted to tell you there had been previous investigators. But Mickey could usually smell it, and he'd worm it out of them. And then he'd be highly annoyed about it and would blow up with me later.

The Diet Coke and the Diet Pepsi came. Mickey made phone calls on his cell phone. I was thinking how hard it had been not to burst out talking when we'd been alone at last, in the elevator, but detectives thought most elevators were bugged and you shouldn't ever say anything in one. On the way to the car Mickey had only one pronouncement: "She's a hooker."

I said, "Don't be silly. She's just got a lot going on."

"Remember I said it, Charlie. She's a hooker."

No, she wasn't. She simply had a stable of sugar daddies. I watched Mickey's face as he talked on the phone across the table from me now. He was right about an awful lot of things. But he was wrong about this. I studied him as he returned calls to this lawyer and that one. He possessed a sexy sort of competence. He isn't that much taller than I am, but I always think of him as much taller because I look up to him.

Mickey put the phone down when the food came. "I can't make him tell me what he wants."

"Because he doesn't know what he wants. He's fascinated by this woman. He can't stand the idea of letting go of her even when she is in the arms of another man." I knew I sounded like a trashy novelist. I felt like one.

We were stunned at the apartments, the real estate he had heaped upon her. Bank accounts and Visa cards, all those telephones and cars. And that was only in this country. Mickey sighed and said, "I don't want to investigate this woman."

"Neither do I," I said sweetly. "I want to take lessons from her."

Mickey was halfway through a bowl of rice pudding when one of his beepers went off, informing him his warrant had been canceled because of the extreme heat. We both went back to the law firm for round two of the meeting with Lo and Yu. This case was to be our little break from chasing counterfeiters. Mickey's present to me. We didn't know it then but this was the summer we were to become slaves of a maniacal Chinese tycoon.

Backout work via computer, via Nynex. Addresses. Everything was in my neighborhood. I was stunned to think of all that could go on within a quarter of a mile in this town. In other places a quarter of a mile was just that, but here we were packed in so tightly that the intrigue was as layered as that delicate pastry I had learned to make at the Cordon Bleu in Rome, *mille foglie*—a thousand leaves. Mickey and I pored over the pages Mr. Yu drowned us in. He'd added notes and arrows and circles.

The office got crowded. As if they knew about our spacious new quarters, we began to get visitors. The old gang from Parker's began to stop by.

This morning Dave was waiting for Mickey, who was out, and instead of going away and coming back later, Dave had decided to stick around and talk.

"So, Dave, what's your job description? What exactly do you call what you do for the NYPD?" I wanted him to talk, so I wouldn't have to and would be able to focus on sorting about thirty faxes chronologically.

"I don't have a title. I look for bodies. I wear scuba gear. Bodies in water. That's it."

"How do you see anything?" I asked. "It must be dark down there."

"It's black. Ya can't see your hand two inches in front a your face. It's black and the silt gets all stirred up which dudn't help any. It's all by touch." He sat down on the edge of my desk, lowering his large bulk slowly, carefully. I anticipated a *crack* noise, but it didn't come. He was wearing a striped, short-sleeved shirt and jeans and running shoes. His face was round and his body matched with a Teddy bear softness, but he rarely smiled, was usually in a bad mood. I wished Mickey would come back.

"So you just keep feeling till you find one. What's the most exciting one you ever had?" I was putting yesterday's faxes in one pile and the twelve that had come today in a second pile. The fax bell rang and I winced. We both turned to look at it as the machine began its purr.

"The best floater I ever saw was a Pepsi Cola salesman. He had two five-bar weights tied with wire around his neck. Each bar is a hundred ten pounds. So he had all that around his neck, but he floated up anyway."

"Oh, wow," I said. I'd heard bodies in water looked particularly horrible.

Dave was excited. "So he surfaced and then a mouse ran out of his mouth." He paused, then announced triumphantly. "I got it all on video."

The door to the hall closed. "Who had a mouse in his mouth?" Mickey demanded.

The phone calls were incessant, the faxes arrived just about every hour. One message scrawled in a margin read "Previous investigator told me this address does not exist." So I walked over to the address, and there it was: a pretty little four-story townhouse complete with window boxes. Snapped a few photos.

I walked home and called Mickey.

"Got a crayon?" he asked and then gave me another address.

We talked awhile. It looked very bad for the The Chin. Mickey turned up the radio in the office so we could both hear the latest newscast: The Chin had once planned to blow up John Gotti with a remote-controlled bomb.

"That's not his style," said Mickey.

"But he hated Gotti's style," I countered. "But did he hate it enough? That's the question." We nattered on about it. I could hear Mickey making little *clicks* on the computer keyboard. Sammy the Bull would take the stand the next day.

Mickey flipped off the radio and started in on Bailey who was mad at him because he was never home. Lovable but deeply troubled. Mickey even hired a dog shrink to come and talk to her. "I know I'm here too much, but I can't seem to get outta here," says Mickey. The other office phone started ringing.

We hung up and I grabbed my Speedo to go for a swim at the pool. When I got back I started returning calls—as many as I could before six. Call waiting clicked and it was Mickey. We agreed that The Chin didn't look well on channel four. A bit pallid. Mickey wanted to appear as a character witness. He was passionate about it. "I used to go and get his Light n' Lively for him, and he'd stick a fifty-dollar bill in my pocket." He'd told me this before, but I never get bored hearing it. Mickey was a baby mobster and may have taken a sabbatical from third grade to fetch milk full-time for the Mafia. I don't ask a lot of questions. He was born in Greenwich Village. I was born in Mississippi. And here we are, hanging around together.

We talked. We cursed Sammy the Bull. Other people were call-waiting us, again and again. We hung up.

A part of me couldn't believe that my partner, one of my best friends in the world, wanted to publicly defend a mobster who was accused of killing a minimum of seven people. Well, that was Mickey for you. The principle is everything. "That trial shouldn't be taking place!" he'd said. "I remember going into his house and seeing him, and this was years ago, talking to himself." Forget the murders. Mickey had been adamant. "He's not fit to stand trial. Once I saw him in the shower with all his clothes on, holding an umbrella. Years ago."

The evening flew. I worked on the computer, talked on the phone, watched a *Seinfeld* re-run at eleven, and got into the sleeping bag. I lay there for twenty seconds and then leapt out of the bag and fumbled for the lamp. I threw pieces of paper all over, searching. The address, the new one Mickey had just given me—*That is where I went to a dinner party two weeks ago!* Just sold, according to Mr. Yu's notes, for $9.5 million. Yes, that was the townhouse my French friends were living in. They'd given their going-away dinner there and then decamped to the Carlyle. The rent was twelve grand per month. I waved the paper in the air dramatically, wishing I didn't live alone.

It was almost midnight but I was so excited that I called Mickey and told him. He nearly laughed.

"I remember asking my friend if the owner was Chinese because of all the Chinese landscapes on the walls, because of the Chinese carved sculptures..." I stopped for air. "And he said no, he wasn't but he loved that part of the world." I was in Alvin's house! "I sat in his living room, I ate at his dining room table!"

"Didn't Mr. Yu say he wants us to go in and take the wedding photograph off the piano?" Mickey asked.

"There isn't any piano for it to be on. The moving vans have been outside—it's right around the corner from me—for the last three days. That house is empty."

"Not in that house—in the apartment!" Mickey could change focus in a millisecond.

"Oh, sure. I'll just go in to that building, which might as well be the Pentagon, and after leveling the doormen in a blaze of machine gun fire, casually push the elevator button and get in, go up, pick the lock and—"

"Stop. I know." Mickey sighed. "Never should have taken this on. It smells like a domestic to me."

A domestic. Bottom of the barrel. We were way beyond domestics. "Look, we'll just do what he wants us to do for another ten days—except no breaking and entering—I won't be happy in jail—and she'll get on that plane for Hong Kong and we'll bill him and he'll pay us. *Finito.*"

This common sense was met with a snort from Greenwich Village.

"Look," I persisted. "We don't really have a choice. If you don't want to talk to him again I will. I don't mind him. I sort of like him. He's passionate and suffering and madly in love—"

"He's obsessive and crazy."

"That, too," I admitted.

Then we discussed whether or not Mr. Yu was paying us to stalk the love of his life. Mickey refused to believe that she *was* the love interest. I refused to believe it was only money. "If he wants the money back then wouldn't he have us do credit checks instead of stakeouts? Wouldn't we be looking at property ownership instead of whether she's letting Alvin drive Claire 2?"

We went on and on. I turned off the lamp and sat in the dark in my nightgown in my wicker desk chair as we enlightened each other with our respective opinions.

"Look, I gotta go walk Bailey. Talk to you in the morning," Mickey said.

We hung up. It *was* morning. I slithered into the bag but it was too hot, so I stood on a stool and stuffed the bag on the top closet shelf with my scarves and the Glock I will never use that Mickey gave me as a Christmas present. It was in a locked box, as law required, with the key in another location, as law required. The bullets were in another locked box, which was hidden in another location, and there was yet another hidden key. Mickey said I needed this paraphernalia for protection. One key was in the dishwasher in my silver evening bag. The other? Not sure where. If someone were breaking in, I'd have to grab a chair, leap on it, fumble under all my silk scarves on the top closet shelf and get the Glock box down. Then I would run to the dishwasher for the pocketbook with the key. Then I'd try to remember where I hid the box of bullets and when I found that I'd have to remember where I put the key. Opening everything, loading the gun and firing would take awhile. I had told Mickey that if anyone broke into the apartment they could make a sandwich, drink a beer, and take a shower after raping me eleven times and I still would not have my hands on the loaded Glock. Now I got off the chair, closed the closet door, and finally found the straw mat with a rubber band around it standing in the kitchen with my broom. I tossed it on the floor and flopped on top of it.

I didn't close my eyes. *My God*, I thought. *I was right there.* Alvin and Lynn. One of the love nests. I was there. It was a block away. I might have seen them in the deli downstairs. They might have seen me. Suddenly

Manhattan seemed about as big and anonymous as Possum Run, Mississippi. I fell asleep and dreamed of the townhouse with the Chinese paintings.

Each of the two rooms over the drugstore was eight by ten and a half feet and guarded by surveillance cameras inside and out. All the walls from floor to ceiling were festooned with the tools of the trade: two-way radios, throw-away phones, reference books, notepads, tape recorders, monitors, video cameras, parkas, hats, and flak jackets. Thirty framed certificates from various law-enforcement agencies gave Mickey their respective stamps of approval. Guns were on the desk mixed in with files or tossed in desk drawers. A baseball bat was propped by the one window. A billy club hung from a leather strap on the door and made a big noise whenever anyone went in or out. This office was prepared for attack.

I flopped into my chair with the flak jacket used as a cushion and handed Mickey a Diet Pepsi, then snapped open my Diet Coke. We didn't usually say hello.

Mickey looked as if he were in pain.

"What?" I asked.

"It's Louie, the three-legged, one-eyed dog. No matter what case it is. Louie always turns up."

I took the folder out of his hand and saw Alvin's business address. *Damn. Damn!* "He's in six seventy-seven . . . !" A counterfeiter! "And maybe that's why Lynn looks so familiar. I've probably seen her down on Canal selling phony Louis Vuitton." I was only half joking.

We were silent. The cell phone on the desk rang and Mickey turned to grab it. "Oh, Mr. Yu," said Mickey, reaching forward to grab a pen.

The cell phone struck again. Our umbilical cord to Mr. Yu. He slept with his phone and would wake up in the night with ideas and would punch out our numbers to talk. Twelve hours' time difference. I had turned off the ringer on my fax machine at home but sometimes would be roused from a dream with the purr that signaled the arrival of a thought from Mr. Yu. He would telephone all day. A call from him at four in the afternoon often meant he had not yet gone to bed but then he would request we call him at seven p.m. or before we left the office and before he went to his. There were car phones and office phones in Kuala Lumpur, in Hong Kong, in Singapore, and the cell, of course, and the answering machine that answered in both Chinese and English. There was a night fax and a day fax. The Chinese was omnipresent.

Mickey spun around to face me. A sort of moveable throne on casters is de rigueur for detectives. "Yes, yes. I understand. Yes, we have that." He was shuffling through papers. "Yes, I did receive three, five, no . . . nine faxes from you today."

"You up?"

"Sure," I tried to sound alert. "I'm on my way to Hertz."

"I'll be at the location at eleven. I've got a radio for you and a phone and a video camera."

I did fifty sit-ups, jumped in and out of the shower, pulled on white shorts and a blue gingham shirt, scuffed my feet into white moccasins that would be better than sandals if I had to drive fast.

The crowd at Hertz was dressed as I was but they carried monogrammed canvas bags full of cheese, wine, and best-sellers. Their shopping bags were from Williams Sonoma. My bag looked like any other, but it contained a sweatshirt, a notebook, pens, a bottle of club soda, a Swiss Army knife, my flashlight. Tic Tacs rattled in three flavors. I was really spoiling myself. What a positively sybaritic life.

In the rental car, I got a good spot, if there was such a thing—the location was a nightmare. Scaffolding over the front entrance covered the entire semi-circular driveway in a forest of steel tinker toys. In the middle of Seventy-Second Street were two Con Ed trucks, and various workers in yellow hard hats climbed in and out of a manhole, which meant I couldn't sit across the street and see anything. Even if the traffic hadn't been a snarling mess, the visibility was ridiculous.

"Take this," Mickey was standing outside my window with a radio in his hand. I always felt lucky that he took care of the technical stuff and was a good explainer. Me—being dragged into the twenty-first century against my will. Me—who used to say a prayer before turning my hair dryer from medium to high because I fully expected it to blow up like a grenade right there in my hand. The men would have loved to call me Three Fingers Charlie. I was one person when I was alone with my hairdryer and another when I was at work. As a detective, I would dissect motion-activated cameras and wear microphones inside my clothes and lean over Mickey, fascinated, as he took apart a .38.

I watched Mickey jaywalk into the traffic. Fearless, a total New Yorker. He got into his car across the street. It looked exactly like a cop car. It was navy blue, the darkest color blue it's legal to be, and it had enough radios and stuff in it to shame mission control in Houston. The windows were as black as they could legally be in New York State, and nobody outside could even see a silhouette at the wheel. The trunk was full of the trappings of the trade—some sophisticated, some not—including a deck chair, which Mickey had been known to whip out and set up right on a city sidewalk in order to catch rays during a stakeout. The Crown Vic, short for Crown Victoria, was equipped to do just about everything but fly.

I stared off to the side as the doorman, like a toy soldier, opened and closed a taxicab door. I checked the rearview mirror. I wondered if I had always secretly been a detective. It was being a little kid playing games. I stared out the window. I wondered what she was like. Irresistible, that goes without saying. Manipulative, witty, fascinating. Wielding power over a powerful man. She had lured him gently, I assumed, from infatuation into the miserable throes of obsession. He gave, she took. And she slept with him and he tried to make her happy the only way he knew how... by writing checks. With her, this powerful man was without power. Bedazzled.

The radio cheeped but I couldn't hear words. I picked it up and squeezed. "Ten-five. Go again."

Mickey's voice. "You're in the best place but the doorman is gonna start worrying about you in a few hours."

"Should I move? Should I go around the block?"

"No. Stay there. I'll tell you when and we'll change places. It's lousy here. Every time a bus pulls up I can't see a thing for at least half a minute." We knew it could all happen in the blink of an eye. When you missed a subject you missed *entirely*.

The doorman often gave that little leap, a mix of being eager and being obsequious, to open a taxi door, to take a package. The Upper East Side. The Gold Coast. Most of the inhabitants, however, resembled refugees from a baseball game that had gone into too many innings. They walked in front of the building with laundry bags, with dry cleaning, with shopping bags from the Gap, with groceries, with little kids. I played the radio, got barefooted and ate Tic Tacs.

We discussed checking on Claire 2 in the multi-storied underground garage but there was no way to do it.

Dozens of people spilled out of that front door. The radio cheeped. Mickey sighed. "Charlie, Mr. Yu is calling the office. He wants my new cell phone number so we can be in constant contact."

I picked up the radio and moaned. "Are you going to give it to him?"

"I checked my machine and he's called four times in the last hour. That doesn't count the faxes I'm in no position to read."

"Doesn't that man ever sleep?" I rolled my eyes.

"I refuse to give him my number."

"What are you gonna tell him about not giving it to him?"

"I'll tell him it's unsafe. We have to use a land line."

"Good. And it's the truth."

Mickey radioed me back. "He's called her six times today, and she told him she took the kids out to breakfast and she's been out shopping in Claire 2."

"Yes, and she's invisible." Between the two of us we could see the front door and the garage entrance and exit, everything on both Second and Seventy-Second. "Or else she's wearing a wig."

Mickey dismissed that. "That's something you'd do but she's normal."

I gave the radio a pained look. "Mickey, she lies."

"I know she lies, you know she lies, Mr. Yu knows she lies."

"Yes. And we could tell him anything and she could tell him anything." I sighed.

"In the end, he'll get tired of us telling him the truth, and he'll choose her and her lies over us because he doesn't want to hear what we'll have to tell him. Then he'll get a new investigator."

I knew how much Mickey hated this case. But I knew he'd hate it more if we were replaced. "Can't he see he's strangling her?" I remember being the object of obsession—a couple of times. It was flattering for the first ten minutes then a nuisance and at last, suffocating. Twice, complete with the silly "if I can't have you, nobody can" death threats.

"I told her he'd be better off letting us watch her instead of calling her to ask where she is, but he can't stop."

"He's forcing her to lie. For oxygen. And if she's not married to him what rights does he have?"

"Don't forget what I told you that first day, Charlie."

"I remember but you're wrong." I thought of money buying somebody. You owe me. I own you. I put down the radio.

Mid-afternoon. It was hot. I brushed my hair up into a French twist, clipped it, and reapplied lipstick, all while never taking my eyes off the front door between rearview-mirror glances at the garage entrance and exit. I had once lost a female subject in Mississippi because I was fooling with mascara in the rearview mirror. Lipstick and hand lotion were now as ambitious as I got in the realm of stakeout beauty rituals. Time passed slowly.

At last! I grabbed my camera and started clicking away, then fumbled for the radio. "Walking east on Seventy-Second! The little girls and the nanny!"

"I got 'em on video. At least this day won't be a total waste." The ever-cool Mickey. I wished I wouldn't get so excited. I spend so much energy trying to fake nonchalance.

The traffic seemed to be actually growling. I radioed Mickey that I was leaving the location for five minutes, put the PRESS sign in the windshield, locked the car and crossed the street to a restaurant. In three minutes I was in the car again, amazed that it took so little—a trip to the ladies' room and clean hands—to cheer me. Then Mickey took a personal, too. He radioed he was back. "You didn't miss a thing," I said and put down the radio. This was easy. A military operation for the spoiled.

I thought of my rural detectivey in Mississippi. Specifically a stakeout with Lyndon in a parking lot off the highway, where the heat rose like heat off a stove. We were waiting for an adulteress to appear and get into a white van and then the plan was to follow her into the next county. My only problem with this was the idea of an adulteress eating at a Red Lobster. I had not yet seen the subject but had imbued her with glamour and panache. It was July. Sweat was pouring off us; my thighs were stuck to the front seat as we drank Dr. Peppers and passed a bucket of popcorn back and forth. I was up to my right wrist in melted butter and my left hand held the cold can of soda to my cheek in between swigs. A river of sweat was running between my breasts, and I'd turned up my shirt collar so as not to feel the hair on my neck. I longed for a rubber band, a ponytail, a crewcut, a shaved head. We'd been in this condition for over two hours when Lyndon turned to me, red-faced and dripping in this hell, and said, "Ya know, it just dudn't get any better than this."

Instead of screaming with laughter, I listened solemnly to his explanation. This is what novices do.

"We've got shelter. We're not out in the rain and we're not out in the sun. There's a restroom nearby and possible food. We're comfortable. This is the best possible situation."

Now only during the most outrageously miserable times did I quote Lyndon to myself: *"It just dudn't get any better than this."*

The hours wore on. Mickey appeared at my window at one point, enraged. "Mr. Yu called and insinuated that I wasn't here!" He was livid.

"You want me to talk to him the next time?" I thought Mickey needed a little respite from the Asian calls.

"No. But the next time he comes to New York I'll get Johnny Lumps to break his ankles for him." Mickey puffed quickly on his Marlboro and then turned and started across the street to his car.

I watched him jaywalk nonchalantly in his faded jeans. *Principle is everything*, I thought. To Mickey, it was. I had taped on the wall above my desk, "Integrity Is All," the family motto of the Rothschilds. It was so easy to tell a lie, to bend the truth. We detectives were paid for being good at it. But for the client to doubt our word? Unthinkable.

Afternoon became evening. Couples appeared, now showered and combed, on their way to restaurants as opposed to grocery stores, hardware stores, and dry cleaners. They walked more slowly than during the day, talked more softly. Where was Lynn? I still hadn't even seen her. Nobody could have spent this entire glorious summer day in an apartment. I flipped the PRESS card in place, locked the car, and went over and slipped into Mickey's front seat. We made a scam call to Lynn's apartment and tried to decide whether it was being call-forwarded. "It rang so many times. Maybe she's . . ."

"Did you hear that little jump, that little change in ring you hear when it's being forwarded?" Mickey asked.

I shook my head. "But I still think she's probably on a porch looking out at blue water sipping champagne."

Mickey lowered his window and lit a cigarette. "Mr. Yu says she's in there. She's been in and out all day. The girls went out to breakfast with her and later to lunch. She told him she might stay in for dinner because she's tired."

I made a cynical noise.

Mickey turned and blew smoke out the window. "That probably means she's going out for dinner after being in all day."

"Unless she's a hundred miles away with call-forwarding."

Evening became night and we stayed, watching, ever-vigilant. Was she watching TV with her kids? Or was she in one of her other apartments in an enormous bed doing unspeakable things to a panting Alvin?

At eleven-thirty, Mickey radioed me to break it off. His car disappeared across town in a flash. I proceeded downtown on Second, then parked on Third. I passed The Sign of the Dove with the outdoor tables occupied by couples chattering and laughing. Brandy balloons. Candles. Piano notes wafted out the open doors. A summer evening. I wondered if Lynn was wearing jade jewelry and pastel chiffon and leaning over a white damask tablecloth flirting with Alvin. Then I imagined them tangled, naked, in scented sheets, surfacing only long enough to toast each other with flutes of champagne. I imagined them laughing at Mr. Yu, helpless in Hong Kong or suspicious in Singapore.

I collected my mail and went up the three flights. I unlocked the door and looked around the room as if I'd been away for months. At first I didn't recognize the shirt over the chair, the sandals. It was as if I'd been in a very long movie and now I were out blinking in the sunlight. It was a curious kind of fatigue mixed with dissatisfaction. The quarry had eluded us.

As I tossed the keys on the bookshelf, the phone rang. Caller I.D. printed that it was "anonymous," but I took a chance and picked it up before my answering machine did.

"Hey, Charlie," barked Mickey. "What are you up to?"

I sank into the green wicker desk chair, and we started to plot the next day.

Sunday morning. That same still heat hung over the city; I walked to the car like a sleepwalker. "I hate to sound like a broken record but if you can use call-forwarding, then so can she. That phone could be answered in Finland," I said.

Mickey was inexplicably convinced she was upstairs. I thought he was dead wrong, but I also knew he had excellent instincts. I was parked in my same place, looking eastward at the location, and Mickey was leaning in my window. "Here's the video camera." He explained how it worked, then let me practice. Simple. I was used to the little one hidden under my clothes but I'd never videotaped in the open. *Terrific*, I think. *One more thing I can do.*

Then Mickey pushed a handful of papers through the window. "These came from Hong Kong last night."

"She looks different in every one," I said, as I fanned through the eight-by-ten black-and-white images. One was a close-up of pouty lips and bouffant hair and said, *Take me to bed this minute.* Another was of her in a low-necked long dress, reclining. Another was an impish schoolgirl minx. The last showed Lynn with hair swept severely back wearing a tight, tailored jacket. "All she needs is a whip," said Mickey.

"She never looks the same twice." Mickey left and went back across the street. Thank God, Con Ed had finished the subterranean tinkering that had disturbed the surveillance of the day before.

I watched the front door, ate six Tic Tacs. Clusters of people crossed Seventy-Second Street. Nobody I'd go to bed with. I wondered how much anyone would have paid for me. I counted the taxis pulling up to the doorman in one part of my brain while my eyes focused only on the door or the rearview mirror. Time passed. Was this a sort of Zen exercise? To aim for "enlightenment by direct intuition through meditation."

Mickey and I changed places. More time passed and we changed again. Then I walked over to his car for a visit and slipped into the front seat, which is why I was with him when we spotted Claire 2, the black Range Rover, as it materialized in the driveway.

"Okay," Mickey said. He grabbed the video camera and started filming. Two heads. A male driving. That's what Mr. Yu wanted to know. Didn't the Beatles sing "Baby, You Can Drive My Car"? But you can't drive Claire 2 if it's registered to Mr. Yu. We pulled away behind them but missed the light. We were in the far left-hand lane and desperately needed to make a right-hand turn across four lanes of traffic on Second Avenue.

The black Range Rover was out of sight heading west. Mickey did just one *whoop* on the siren. We pulled across all four lanes at the red light, and then the westbound traffic across Seventy-Second parted like the Red Sea in the Bible.

We watched them turn onto Park and followed them directly to Alvin's townhouse—where I'd been to the dinner party. Mickey said Alvin had a fat ass and I nodded. He was six feet tall with white hair, but his face was impossible to see. Then, with the camera going, Mickey said, "She's beautiful," and I whipped around to look at him. Was he saying that on tape for Yu's benefit or did he mean it? I looked at her through my camera lens. At last. Round face, no cheekbones to speak of. That jet-black, shining, straight hair with bangs. Her breasts were pushed up and out of the scoop-necked orange tank top, and her jeans were so tight they looked as if they might hurt. She was strictly K-Mart sartorially. Mickey turned off the video camera and said, "Chubby, isn't she?"

We followed them back to the apartment building and watched the doorman help them unload a few pieces of furniture. Claire 2 nipped into the garage like a rabbit, and Mickey parked in front.

This woman drove men wild. I thought of Mr. Yu's shock when Piggy had presented him with the photos of the man he expected to be Alvin and instead her escort was an unidentified Japanese. I thought of "the Jewish American" and wondered all sorts of things. Why did she pick him over Mr. Yu? He had money but nobody had as much money as Mr. Yu. Maybe Lynn wanted security and marriage. But she'd had that. She was a widow with children. I wondered what she had that I didn't have—not counting three apartments, ten cell phones, and real estate holdings on at least two continents. What tricks of the Orient? What did she want, I wondered, that she didn't already have?

Mickey suddenly turned to me in the front seat. "So what do you think, Charlie? What does Mr. Yu really want from us?"

* * *

On Monday we FedExed the videos of both days to Kuala Lumpur. We were in the office discussing the double-dealing doorman, sure that both Mr. Yu and Lynn were paying him. The phone rang. Mickey talked to a lawyer about a counterfeit case, while I looked through the Yu file.

Mickey hung up and the phone rang again. He snapped up the receiver giving me the "It's him" look. "Good morning—no, good evening, Mr. Yu."

When he hung up, I said, "I still don't get it. She isn't married to him. He called me the other day and told me that when he calls her she sometimes begs him to marry her. Why doesn't he? He told me he's divorced. He's free. She's free. Why doesn't he get her away from Alvin once and for all?"

Mickey swung around in his chair. "Divorced?"

"Yep. He said it was 'five-year expiration plan.'"

"Well, he told me his wife is an invalid. And there are certain fax machines and certain phone numbers we aren't to use at night."

"What!" I shouted. "He lied to me! I cannot believe this!"

Mickey had that smirk on his face I knew so well. Then he spun around to return to his report. I addressed his profile. In the car, in the office, I usually talked to the right side of his face. "I know what you're thinking!"

"What, Charlie?" I could hear the smirk. He was goading me.

"I'll tell you what! When I lie during a case it's professional prevarication. Necessary deception. I never lie in real life! Absolutely never! And Mr. Yu lying to me is real life! I am shocked."

"Stop being shocked and look at this. Tell me if you see anything . . ." He handed me a bank statement from Citibank.

I took a deep breath. "Chinatown branch. I love it already." I opened the folded pages; it was Lynn's statement from May. "Did *you* see this?"

"Came in the mail half an hour ago. Haven't had time."

The phone rang and I picked it up. "Investigations." Pause. "Oh, Mr. Yu, how are you?" We talked about Lynn. "What about the health club?

It's right there in the building."

No, he said, she didn't like to exercise. "This next weekend very important," he said. "Her last weekend before she come to Hong Kong. She very busy. You and Mickey must watch carefully."

"I understand," I said, nodding. When I could break in, I did. "Mr. Yu, Mickey just handed me a bank statement, and there's a deposit in May for two million five hundred thousand dollars. Where did that come from? Did she sell property?"

"Oh, that not really her money," came the response from the other side of the world. "I put in when she tell me she little short on cash."

The same old story. Five million to help her with the Hong Kong bank problem. The Visa cards. The phones. One apartment purchased, then another and then another. The summer house. And just this spring she'd asked him if he wanted to buy one of the apartments back from her because she was "a little short on cash." Mr. Yu, for all his chopped English, was a beautifully educated man. He'd been to the best schools in England and had a degree from Harvard. But Suzi Wong was playing games with him—and winning.

"Just want say one thing." I waited. His voice was solemn. "Want to say that she know I have dip pockets."

Mr. Yu might have "dip pockets," but I didn't and Mickey didn't. On the Lexington Avenue bus the next day I wondered about being a concubine. For whom would I concubine? I doubted Match.com would be a resource for this. The bus wheezed along. A great elephant in the traffic. The bus took forever but Mickey had warned me not to take the subway this week. Something about germ warfare. Inside information only he and his pal Chiefie had. Sometimes I thought those two characters were tapping into Pentagon intelligence sources. They wanted me to think that. They loved being mysterious, loved having me plead with them to tell me more. Chiefie would smile; Mickey would smirk, They teased me, and sometimes I even stamped my foot in outrage, but to no avail. I never knew when they were having me on. So here I was on the Lexington Avenue bus as it crawled downtown in the rush hour traffic.

I got off at Thirty-Fourth Street, walked toward Park, bought some bubble bath in the drugstore, and then went outside to the other door of the building and went up in the elevator. Mickey's two doors were both locked, so I banged on the first one, then looked up at the camera and made a face. The door snapped open and there stood Louie, one of the narcs of the NYPD. Bailey howled in greeting. The room was crowded even with the hole in the wall giving a sense of space beyond.

Louie was African American, just my height at five foot nine, and slender. Really built. Muscles moved under his T-shirt when he lifted a cup of coffee. "Charlie, where's your gas mask?" demanded Mickey from his desk in the corner.

"I didn't take the subway today."

"I gave her a mask for Christmas," Mickey said to Louie.

"And a Glock," I added.

"Gas mask?"

"Yeah, well, you know the next attack will be gas released in the subway system." Mickey was tapping on the computer.

Louie laughed, "Hey, man! Where'd you hear that?"

"I didn't have to hear it. I know it. It's obvious," stated Mickey. "And Charlie takes the subway all the time and should protect herself." He turned to me where I stood on the other side of the hole in the wall. "Ya gotta keep it with you all the time, Charlie."

I put my head and one shoulder through the hole. "I can't carry it around, Mickey. It's as big as a bowling ball."

Louie looked at me. "Where is it?"

"It's at home. In the dishwasher."

"The dishwasher?" they chorused.

"Yeah, I keep my evening bags on the little racks at the top where you put glasses and the gas mask is where you put plates."

"Don't use it much?" said Louie grinning.

"Never used it," I said going back through the hole in the wall.

I heard Mickey. "Because she never cooks."

"Not true," I called back. "I make popcorn all the time. Four times a week. Minimum."

Mickey was speaking in a low voice. "Yeah, and she doesn't believe in microwaves so she uses hot oil and wears sunglasses for protection."

"I heard that!" I shouted. "It's common sense!"

Louie started laughing, Bailey started barking, and the phone rang.

It was a baking day after a sultry night. I'd gotten off the floor at three a.m. and actually considered moving several dozen books from the window sill which would mean I could turn on the air conditioner. Considered it. Then walked into the bathroom and stood under a cool shower still considering it. I stepped out of the bathroom and, dripping wet, sat on the floor in front of the fan until I felt deliciously chilled and could lie down again and sleep.

I walked into the office and Mickey handed me a sheet of notebook paper. Three new Broadway locations..." Mickey was tapping on the computer, talking to me in profile as usual.

"Two guys. I know 'em both," Mickey said. "Big shots at a pricey firm charging huge hourly fees and they blew it." I knew what firm he meant. I'd done work for them. They were a Kroll-wannabe outfit.

"When do they want you to do this?" I asked, reading the addresses.

"Yesterday."

There was a bang on the door, Mickey opened it about five inches and handed out a few bills. There was barely enough room to take in the paper bag. I heard somebody say, "Gracias," and the door closed. The phone rang and Mickey talked to a client as we both snapped open our diet sodas. I went through the hole in the wall and sat down in the other room, and listed all I had to do. The counterfeit locations were new.

I was holding myself back, stalling. The previous investigators had screwed up, so everyone at the location would be hinky before I opened my mouth. Sometimes I felt like an actress who hadn't seen the script. I'd be pushed onto the stage and the curtain would rise, so to speak, when I walked in the door. It was quite a feeling. Adrenalin. My drug of choice.

Summer on Fifth Avenue. Lots of tourists wearing shorts and sandals, dragging shopping bags, business types wearing ties, dragging briefcases.

I did the locations then called the office from a phone booth on Fifth, but Mickey had left for his meeting uptown, so I headed home. I was halfway down the stairs to the subway when I remembered the warnings, so I began to walk uptown instead, talking to myself. A few hours later, clean, and lying on my straw mat, I fell asleep thinking of Mr. Yu's lying to me.

Seven o'clock the next morning and the phone rang in my apartment. "He just called," Mickey said. I didn't have to ask who "he" was. "She told him she's going to be with her trainer—suddenly she's got a trainer—at seven-thirty."

"At the club? You want me over there? Right." I was wondering where my sneakers were. I pictured myself on a treadmill beside Lotus Blossom in Lycra. "No photos? Well, what's the point then? What does he want?"

"I don't know, Charlie. I just told him I'd have one of my investigators over there."

One of his investigators. There were four of us. Chiefie was smooth, very cool but he smoked too much and now had one lung or maybe less, so he was more useful in the car and on the computer than in the field. He is known as Froggy on the radio but as Chiefie in person. Chiefie told a lot of good stories and delivered them in an indescribable voice. I sensed that Chiefie had quite a past and that it was being fed to me in little tidbits. One hors d'oeuvre at a time during stakeouts and tails. Bert worked in a hospital doing who knows what and had been known to put on dark glasses and tap around locations with a white cane. Clarkson lived in Harlem and was a large person with muscles on his muscles. He told us about people being

155

thrown off rooftops and shot on the way down with other people shooting up at them as they fell. Then, just in case they were not entirely Swiss-cheesed and dead on arrival, there was somebody standing by, waiting to finish them off. Clarkson didn't *do* it but he knew how it was done. Even though he appeared to witness a dozen homicides a day he exuded a deep serenity.

So it was me and Chiefie and Clarkson and Bert. Usually. Mickey said he didn't trust anybody else. Just us. Hand-picked. Loyal. And capable—most of the time.

"Well, I'm it. I better get out of here. Talk to you later."

"Charlie! One last thing. Her trainer's name is Becky. She's short with long blond hair."

"Yeah, okay, thanks. He told you that? How does he know?"

"Because *she* told him that a few minutes ago on the phone."

I moaned, then hung up, and in five minutes I was out the door walking down Third singing that song I couldn't get out of my mind. Mr. Yu's theme song, "Every Breath You Take."

"Never showed. No Lynn. No Alvin. There is a Becky, but her first two appointments canceled, so I never saw her either. I combed the whole place." I stood at a club pay phone.

"I'll tell him. Thanks, Charlie."

Faxes continued to arrive by the dozen. With the ringer off I only heard only the purr a few feet from my head at night. The last thing I did before getting on my mat was to turn off my phone. In the morning I'd play the messages from a frantic-sounding Mr. Yu dictating a new possible phone number for "her" or an old possible address for "him." This man was definitely "high energy" level. I felt his grip across the Pacific. But my experience was nothing compared to Mickey's. He was drowning in faxes, going deaf from phone messages, going bankrupt with the callbacks, which were nearly impossible to keep track of. We were the lackeys of this mad Chinese.

Mickey would call me with new info. "Got a crayon?"

"Go," I'd say and start to write.

We weathered the insistence that we get the wedding photograph of Lynn and Alvin. Did it exist? Where was the piano it supposedly sat upon? We talked Mr. Yu out of having us impersonate movers to steal the box it was packed in. It was too late, we told him. Well, then, he thought we should become interior decorators and insinuate ourselves into the apartment to help unpack said boxes. It was slapstick, insane. Mickey and Chiefie got plenty of play out of all this with tilted heads and fluttering hands. They lisped me right out of the office.

We had other clients, other cases, other confusion in our lives. Andrew Cunanan was the subject of a massive manhunt in the Versace murder case, and we yakked about possibilities, probable hiding places. Benny Eggs had taken the Fifth and refused to testify against The Chin. We cheered old Benny Eggs as we listened to the evening news together on the phone. Mickey remembered him as a neighborhood character. Sometimes I wondered if I didn't feel slightly jealous of Mickey's childhood. I had been catching lightning bugs and lying in the grass finding faces in clouds when Mickey had already been *really* living. There wasn't any Mafia presence in my neighborhood. I didn't know what a pizza was till I was sixteen. It took me decades to realize that Dean Martin was not singing, "When the moon hits your eye like a big piece of pie." I thought pecan.

The week went by and on that Friday a federal jury convicted The Chin of racketeering and conspiracy to commit murder. "My father called and he's really depressed," said Mickey that afternoon. It was the end of the road for The Chin.

The weekend loomed. "Very busy," Mr. Yu had emphasized.

"What does 'busy' mean? Shopping all weekend? In bed?"

Mickey said, "Remember when I said she was a hooker and you said no? Well, today I had a long talk with Mr. Yu . . ." We were both worn out with the case. It was nearly midnight and our fifth phone call together of the evening. Mickey went on. "I tried to tell him that maybe Alvin was a threat to him. That maybe Alvin was using Lynn to get information about his business."

"So you suggested the treachery of Alvin," I said. "What was his reaction?"

"He didn't think much of my idea." He sighed. "He called Alvin a pimp."

"Really?" I paused. "Do you think his English—"

"Yes. He knows what it means. Alvin is sending Lynn out. She's a hooker." I heard Bailey bark in agreement.

"Remember that awful moment when we were at the law firm and Mr. Yu said something like 'What kind of a man would send his wife to sleep with another man for money?'"

"Yep. That's what's going on. That's why she needs those extra apartments. That's why she probably tips the doormen at her building a pile of cash every month."

I was quiet, considering this. "Well, you're right again."

There was silence, then I could hear him smirking down in Greenwich Village. "Yeah, Charlie. When are you gonna learn to yield to my expertise?"

It was Saturday and it was hot. Without a breeze. A dead-air kind of heat. Mickey and I parked again, then endured the same kind of waiting with video and still cameras on the seat beside us, swigging diet sodas, taking personals, with the occasional radioing back and forth. Time passed.

I thought of Mr. Yu in Hong Kong and placed him in a fabulously modern glass house overlooking Repulse Bay. He was talking loudly, excitedly on a cell phone, wearing a red silk dressing gown and an ascot. His wife would be in a wheelchair, tended by servants, in a faraway wing of the spectacular cliffside house.

The monotony of Saturday afternoon was broken by the arrival of Chiefie in his official-looking car, sleek and black—the antenna farm. I put the PRESS card on my dashboard and went over to say hello.

Mickey had hurt his back a few weeks earlier. He was on the sidewalk explaining this to Chiefie. "It was some kind of sticky Chinese food. I slipped and fell off a dumpster. In Queens. In the middle of the night."

Chiefie said, "I met a doctor at the bowling alley last week. But he's not a real doctor. He said he was sociopathic." Mickey looked at me, daring me to laugh. I stared right back and said, "My psychic knows a faith healer in New Jersey."

Mickey put his head in his hands. Chiefie offered me a stick of Juicy Fruit and I took it.

Then Morris, one of Chiefie's pals, arrived in the same kind of car as Chiefie's and stood with the three of us quite openly. Morris is big. No matter what he does he has to do it quite openly. Later Mickey told me that the only reason nobody had called 9-1-1 or bothered us was that our presence was so obvious they thought we were part of a police action.

We never saw the girls. Nor Lynn. Nor Alvin. Mr. Yu, who now had Mickey's cell phone number, called incessantly. "I just call her and she say that the kids go to pool. Swimming."

I told Mickey it was not possible. "They don't allow children except from six to eight p.m. on Saturday and Sunday."

Then we decided that maybe there could be an exception, and that I'd better check it out, so I rushed upstairs. No, I was told, no children had been in the pool all day.

We went through the usual changing of the doormen at four. Then at five Mickey radioed that we should meet and talk about what to do. We drove downtown, and when he turned left on Fifty-Seventh I followed him to Sutton Place. We parked and he got out and came to stand beside my open car door. The air was heavy with the heat. My cotton shirt and shorts looked as if I'd spent the night on a train. This end of Fifty-Seventh Street was empty, quiet. The occasional doorman under the distant awning looked weighed down by the weather, by the boredom, by his very epaulets.

Mickey stood over me and lit a cigarette, then said it for the hundredth time: "I don't know what Mr. Yu really wants. He says stick with it. I told him she lied about the kids going swimming. She lied about going out shopping, about lunch." He sighed, took a puff of the cigarette, then exhaled smoke. "We are victims of jerkumstance, Charlie."

I kicked off my shoes as I sat in the front seat and turned to put my bare feet out of the open door of the car. My feet looked good; I adore pedicures. "Yes, we are. And she's a liar. And we're the hired help." I splashed club soda out of a bottle on my bare legs. "She lied to buy herself an hour or two without his calling her."

Mickey made a face. "These Asian men can be so horrible about women. He said to me that she had to go to the gym to get in shape for when she came to Hong Kong to be with him." Mickey was clearly disgusted. "'Because with me,' he said, 'she know she must perform.'"

I didn't say anything. Mickey blew smoke out of his nose angrily. It was hot. Manhattan seemed still and silent around us. The cell phone rang and Mickey and I both stared at it in his hand. Before he could answer, it stopped. Hong Kong to Fifty-Seventh Street. There was no escape. We looked at each other and started laughing. At nothing. At everything. The tiredness and the tedium had gotten to us. "Summit at Sutton Place," I said.

"He is sure she go out to dinner tonight."

I started laughing again. "You sound like English is your second language!"

Mickey grinned. He was flushed with the heat, wearing jeans and a plaid shirt and running shoes. Every once in a while he'd fumble for a pager at his belt and then look down and read it. "A fire at Ninety-Eighth and Madison," he reported and clipped it back into place next to his gun.

"If we leave then she will go out to dinner or she'll say she went out to dinner," he said.

"But she could say she went out to dinner and *not* go out to dinner and we'd just sit here and then we'd end up telling Mr. Yu that she never came out and never went out to dinner," I said.

"But then again she might go out, and we wouldn't see her if we weren't there, and we wouldn't get the pictures, and I can't charge him if we're not there, and if I don't charge him he'll know we broke it off, and he wants us to stay, and she'll say she went out to dinner, and he'll say we missed her and didn't get the photos, and he'll be upset." We looked at each other and started laughing again.

"It doesn't matter what we say because she can say anything and it doesn't matter if it's true or not." I sighed.

"I think it's coming down to one thing. Either I tell him that I cannot, in good conscience, continue the surveillance and waste his money or—"

I interrupted, "But he won't like that because he wants us to stay and he doesn't care how much it costs."

"Or we please him by saying we are staying and we leave anyway, and I find a way to not charge him for this without his knowing it." Mickey looked pained.

I looked at that face and thought that ninety-nine out of a hundred detectives in the Yellow Pages would have told the client they were staying—then gone home, taken a shower, had a beer, and charged him anyway. We debated over whether to call him at all and then decided not to wake him up. I was reminded of parents with a cranky baby.

"Look, maybe there's a compromise. Give me the phone. Let's go home. It's nearly seven o'clock. I don't think she's in the building. She's in Southampton with everybody else," I said.

"I think she's upstairs."

"Yeah, but you always think she's upstairs, and I always think she's somewhere else and . . . and actually you were right last weekend." I fumble for a Tic Tac and about twenty fly out onto the street.

"You shouldn't eat those, Charlie. They're not good for you."

He was smoking a Marlboro. I laughed.

"What good will it be for you to answer the phone instead of me?"

"Because you're tired of him and I don't blame you and also because I'll run down the stairs and won't answer it until I get out on Lexington and he'll hear the traffic and think we're on the scene."

Mickey reluctantly agreed and gave me the phone. I knew that part of the reason was Bailey. The rug was in bad shape. We left. I felt odd about it. We weren't really being honest, but we couldn't stay for all those hours again and have nothing happen. Or could we? We should have, but we physically could not. Oh, yes, we could. I'd been lots more tired than this. I resolved to go home, wash my face, call Mickey on a land line, and tell him I was going back.

I parked on Third and walked past The Sign of the Dove again. Everyone looked so clean. I had that same "Did I flee before Vesuvius?" feeling when I opened my apartment door. I recognized nothing at first. A lifetime had passed. The apartment phone rang and I answered. It was Stephan the Frenchman from the second floor. I told him I wasn't supposed to be there, that I was on a case. I told him I'd love to have a drink but I couldn't because I was supposed to be somewhere else and that it was complicated. He laughed, and the cell phone rang. I shouted that I had to hang up and I ran down the stairs, past his doorway, with the phone ringing in my hand. Three flights of stairs and then I flew out the front door like Kramer on *Seinfeld* and in the middle of the sidewalk, panting, answered, "Hello?"

I gulped for air, then held the phone over my head so that it could pick up the noise of the traffic as the light on the corner of Sixty-Fifth turned to green. "No, Mr. Yu. No sign of her. Yes, same place. It's a lousy location because the doormen have been noticing us all day. And I know you know about the construction work."

I held the phone over my head again like a flag when the light changed and then brought it down to my ear and started talking again. "Yes, we're here. No. Call anytime." I closed the phone and turned. It was then that I saw Stephan, immaculate in his navy blazer and white linen trousers, right out of *GQ*, watching me from a sidewalk table in front of Sel et Poivre. I looked at him, waved the phone stupidly, looked down at my bare feet, and then dashed for my front door and up the stairs. When I got up there Mickey was on the line talking to my answering machine. I picked up. "It's okay. Nothing is happening. But maybe in an hour I'll go back."

He said he would go back and I said no, I will. Then the cell phone rang again, and I shouted and hung up on Mickey. I ran down the stairs again two at a time, all three flights and Kramered right out the front door, nearly flattening Johnny from the deli next door. I ran an extra fifteen feet to the corner and opened the phone. "Yes, Mr. Yu. No, I . . . uh . . . I didn't hear it at first. There's very bad traffic noise." I waved the phone over my head again as the light changed and someone obligingly honked for the benefit of those in Hong Kong.

"She go to dinner soon. She take children to movie and to dinner. She leave in five minutes."

I closed the phone and turned to run back to my apartment. Johnny was standing in the doorway of the deli staring. "You okay?" he asked. Stephan was four yards farther away sipping wine, looking handsome and sophisticated. And he was looking at me. I just shook my head and ran past, barefooted, through the front door, scampered up the three flights, and grabbed the phone to call Mickey. I punched in star 82 then his seven-digit number and then my four-digit call blocker unlocker and got his machine. I left the message that I was going back to the location, that she was on her way out to dinner. Then I pulled on sneakers, didn't stop to tie them, and grabbed my bag and the keys, ran down the three flights of stairs, leapt out the front door, and ran around the corner toward Third. I saw in my mind's eye—only a blur—Stephan holding a glass of wine and staring in my direction. I had the radio in my hand and called Mickey as I sprinted along Sixty-Fifth. No answer. In minutes I was in the rented green Mustang racing up Third.

The cell phone rang again on the front seat, and I answered it as I sped past Sixty-Ninth Street. "Yes, Mr. Yu. Well, you know how it is. If she said she was leaving and trying to get out the door maybe she just doesn't want to answer again." I wished desperately for her to be stuck in the elevator. I stopped at the light and tried to concentrate. I was one-half a minute away from the parking place. Mickey was walking Bailey, and I didn't have the video camera, just the still with the damn flash. Instantly alerting anyone and everyone. I suddenly thought. *She's done it again! She's fooled us all, and we're running around like idiots!*

I parked and called Mickey on the cell phone in between calls from Hong Kong. No answer. No one coming out the front door with black hair. I cursed myself for having no video camera, and then I called Mickey on the radio. No answer. Would he take the radio to walk Bailey? Maybe. I realized my radio was low on power. Battery was gone. I called his cell phone. No answer. I called him at home again on the cell phone and got the answering machine. I said damn about eight times as I riveted in, laser-like, on the front door with my mud-brown eyes. Then I started saying damn again because, dammit, she'd done it again! She cheated; she lied. This game being played out across the world was going on far too long. The phone rang. *Damn! Hong Kong again.* "Mr. Yu?" Then I gasped with relief. It was Mickey. "Listen, Mr. Yu call and tell me she out the door. Movie and dinner with children." Burst of laughter from him. Then I realized I sounded like Mr. Yu.

"I'm on my way."

"Wait! You don't have to come because she's not going anywhere. Remember she's been swimming today and out shopping and out for breakfast and for lunch and she's lying. We are stupid, stupid, stupid because we keep believing her."

In minutes Mickey materialized at my window. He must have used the *whoop whoop* siren to get out of the Village that fast. I handed him my radio, and he twisted a recharged battery into the bottom and handed it back.

"It's a bit late to be taking those kids to the movies. I'm nobody's mother, but I think it is. And then dinner afterward? The movie won't be out until ten at this rate. I don't believe this story either." Mickey agreed that it was late to take kids to the movies. We, parents of nobody, were self-righteously outraged at this bad mother.

Mickey returned to his car across the street, and then it began to happen. We saw the kids and the nanny. They played under the porte cochere. A Maserati pulled into the driveway and stopped by the front door. Was it dark blue or black? The lighting was so bad. A man was in the back seat, and there was a chauffeur at the wheel. The man had a Vandyke beard and looked like somebody who'd deal in stolen art.

"Can you see the tag, Charlie?"

"No, not yet," I radioed back, hating the scaffolding.

We were both remembering that last Sunday the kids came out first and she materialized after their appearance.

Suddenly we saw her. Mickey was across Seventy-Second and I was on Second Avenue. She was wearing a long black dress and her hair was curly. No. "It's not Lynn. Or is it?" I radioed.

"It's not Alvin; that's for sure."

"She looks taller. Could be very high heels."

I put down the radio and stared as hard as I could. The driver was walking around the Maserati as if waiting. The man in the back seat got out. A taxi pulled up and dispensed passengers. I couldn't see the woman. The waiting was interminable. The kids went inside. The driver got in and backed up the Maserati, then leapt out and helped the woman into the car; the man who was not Alvin got into the back seat on the other side. "That's her!" radioed Mickey. I started my motor and flipped on my lights.

Green light. *Where do I go? Do I pull through the intersection and go to the right or to the left?* No way to know. I was in the left lane so it would be easier to turn left, and I did it, then pulled up past Mickey's car. I was upset that they might pull out on Seventy-Second and go west when I was heading east—*dammit!* And so was Mickey. I'd screwed it up. If they went west both of us would have to make U-turns in heavy traffic. There was a hold-my-breath moment when the Maserati hesitated on the lip of the driveway and then pulled out to the left and headed east on Seventy-Second

Street. I was so close I saw her face in the back seat as they passed me. She'd curled her hair and was very made up. She stared straight ahead. *Wonder what she is thinking. Is it that lamb-to-the-slaughter feeling or "Thank God for variety"?*

I let them pass me. Mickey was behind me. Then he passed me as we headed toward York Avenue. We all stopped at the light and then turned right, going south. The Maserati zigged and zagged all over the East Side. The sleek little car changed lanes, waiting till the last second to make a turn, never using a blinker.

Mickey radioed, "I'm dropping back. Stick with them. Just let me know where you are."

They were three cars ahead of me, which was perfect for a tail, and we were all heading across Fifty-Seventh Street. It was a lovely night. Cool air was blowing in my window, and I was talking to Mickey with the radio in my right hand and steering with my left, and I was so happy. Manhattan. What a lovely grid. This was my home territory. For once I wasn't worried about missing the exit to Jersey City or that the subject would turn off into downtown Baltimore. A light. Would I make it? Would they turn? "Still going across Fifty-Seventh, passing Third. Now I'm stopped for the light. It's green. We're crossing Lexington. Still headed west," I told Mickey.

"I'm at Fifty-Seventh and Madison, waiting for you."

I loved it. I felt thrilled right down to my painted toenails.

We chased the Maserati over to Madison, and it went uptown, and then it turned onto Park and then went down Park and then onto Madison again, and we went up to Fiftieth, where the Maserati stopped in front of the Palace Hotel. Mickey and I both pulled over to the curb across the street, south of Fiftieth, and we watched them get out and the Maserati pull away.

I pulled out and headed up Madison. "There's a bar in there," I said on the radio. "But I can't go in there like this and look for them."

"Do you look that bad?"

"I look like I barely survived a shipwreck."

"What else is new?"

I made a face. "I could go home and change my clothes."

"Would that help?"

I scowled at the radio. "I'm right at Sixty-Third. We know where they are. You want me to pull on a dress and go in after them?"

It was agreed that I'd park somewhere, go to my apartment, and change and Mickey would pick me up and we'd speed back to the Palace. I ran up the stairs, started the bath water, yanked off my clothes, and leapt into the tub as I fumbled with my watchband. Then I was out and pulling a dress over my head and scuffing into sandals. I grabbed a silver necklace and earrings in my fist but then couldn't find my keys and whirled around in a frantic circle wondering if more than two minutes had gone by. I spotted the keys, grabbed them, slammed the door behind me, and ran down the stairs. Mickey was parked right out front. After I was in the car and we were heading down Lexington, I groaned. Mickey turned to me and asked, "What's the matter? Did you forget something?"

"Sort of." I pulled up the hem of my dress and there written on my thigh was the plate number of the Maserati written in green felt-tip pen. "I took a bath and now it's blurry," I told him.

"You had time to take a bath?" I could count on the fingers of one hand the times Mickey had shown surprise. He laughed into the radio. "Hey, Froggy, she's got the plate written on her thigh! She took a bath and it's coming off!"

Froggy rasped something back. We were now speeding down Lexington, then turning onto Park to let me out at a side entrance on Fifty-First Street. I brushed my hair and clipped on the necklace and earrings.

A doorman with military bearing swung open the door for me, and I thought maybe I didn't look too bad. The carpet felt ankle deep, and the voices were muted. Uniformed porters and a concierge watched me pass the check-in area. Someone was playing a piano about a hundred feet away on an island of marble floor. Three couples at little tables. I went up an enormous staircase, checked the ladies' room. and came down again. I asked a porter where the bar was, and he pointed me up again. I climbed the stairs again. Closed paneled door. It had changed. This was the bar for Le Cirque and not the dark, sexy bar I remembered. I couldn't push the door open and go in there. I went downstairs again and found the entrance to Le Cirque, but I saw someone I knew and wanted to avoid an awkward encounter, so I went back upstairs, checked the ladies' room again, and then left the hotel. I slipped into the front seat beside Mickey.

"Bet anything he's taken her to Le Cirque. I'd forgotten it's there now so they have to be in Le Cirque unless he's taken her directly to bed upstairs."

Mickey looked at his watch. "Nine o'clock. Saturday night. Drinking now and eating in a few minutes."

"We should give them at least two hours to eat since it takes about three months to get a reservation." Mickey turned to look at me. I was very wound up. "I couldn't go in. I wondered if I could slither past the maître d' and get a glimpse of the dining room, but Sirio Maccioni was near the entrance, wearing a dinner jacket, and I know him, for Pete's sake! I was writing a novel about a restaurant a couple of years ago, and he was so nice to me. He took me to lunch. He answered all my questions. He even let me work in the kitchen of the old Le Cirque with the dessert chef. I can't suddenly materialize now and say, 'Oh, I'm a detective now.'"

Mickey stared at me, almost said something, then didn't. "Let's wait it out. Haven't heard from Mr. Yu in twenty minutes. I'm worried."

We parked across Madison, and Mickey took videos of the long, tall windows on the southwest corner of the hotel. I was remembering my short career as a dessert chef and how the executive chef had fired me for not sleeping with him. Then there was the CIA station chief in Rome who had made me the focus of his insane obsession. My friends and I called him Mad Mentor. Then there was my Welsh fiancé stealing all my jewelry and absconding in the middle of the night from Larnaca. Well, actually all the flights from Cyprus seemed to be in the middle of the night, so anyone absconding there always did it in the middle of the night. He is still wanted by Interpol. All this was floating through my mind when I said, "You know, Mickey, with all I've been through, it's a miracle I have a job and am leading a normal life."

Mickey's reply was immediate. "You don't have a job, and no one would ever describe your life as normal."

I didn't answer, but I pulled up my hem and examined a "2" that might have been a "Z." Froggy was on the radio. "So what are you and Madda Harry up to now?"

Mickey and I yakked to Froggy and then settled down in the front seat, staring across Madison at the windows of the elegant restaurant. We were both starving, but we didn't say it. I thought of Popeye Doyle and his partner during the *French Connection* movie when they're eating hot dogs in the car as they watch the subject, through a restaurant window, eating course after gourmet course and drinking champagne. Mickey remembered a great New Year's Eve in the hotel. Nurses. I thought about the restaurant novel that didn't get published. Then about Lynn. "She's forty-two? She looks terrific tonight," I say. "Isn't her birthday soon? In August?"

Mickey said that her birthday was around Christmas. "Her DOB is something like twelve fifteen fifty-five."

I disputed this and then realized my mistake. "I'm thinking of another DOB. The woman raped in the mental hospital case. Sorry."

Mickey started to laugh and said, "She'll prob'ly show up later tonight." We were punchy again. "She's a hooker, Charlie. That is probably some Japanese businessman that Alvin set her up with."

"Maybe she dumped Alvin for the night. Maybe they fought." Why did I want this to be about love and not money? Then I reconsidered. "No. This can't be a spur-of-the-moment Saturday dinner—you can't just walk in and ask for a table at Le Cirque."

We wondered if they'd gone directly upstairs. Wouldn't that be a bit crass after getting all dressed up? I reluctantly conceded that I didn't know how this worked.

"Alvin sent her out with that businessman to sleep with him." Mickey was sure. "Maybe he's Japanese. Maybe he's the same Japanese businessman Piggy saw. Alvin's back waiting for her. He uses her. I tell you, Charlie, I'm right."

"Well, you've been right a lot lately, , so maybe you're right about this, too." I turned on the light and studied the marks on my leg again. "I think it's a z for *zebra*."

Mickey laughed and wrote it on his pad. We started laughing. At nothing. Because we were tired.

At one in the morning they hadn't come out and there was still no sign of the Maserati. I went in again and dared to push open the heavy door to look at the bar area. Within four feet from me was a long, low table, where three very well-tended, middle-aged blondes in black dresses were drinking after-dinner liqueurs. Little plates of fancy cookies sat in front of them, untouched. I coveted them. I let the door whisper closed and descended the stairs again.

In minutes I was in the front seat with Mickey. "No, didn't see her. Checked the bar and the ladies' room again." We talked about strategy, covered all the maybes. A driver and car was hired to take them from the apartment to the hotel? Or was it Alvin's Maserati? Were they finished for the evening? We called Mr. Yu, who was pleased to hear from us and wanted us to wait for her to come out and to follow her wherever. Mickey sighed a lot during the conversation, then hung up and said, "We know she is with Alvin, with this other man, that she lies to him. What else does he want us to find out?" The case had proceeded day after day with so much unanswered.

Mickey called Mr. Yu back and persuaded him that it was time to break it off. Mickey drove me home, and in four minutes I'd brushed my teeth, unplugged my phone, and fallen asleep on the straw mat.

I dreamed I was in a car driving in darkness behind two red tail lights and I could never quite catch up. I grabbed my radio from the front seat, squeezed it, and called for Mickey. No answer. The batteries were dead. I drove on through an empty, black nightscape.

In the morning I listened to the messages that Mickey had left at one-thirty and at two. "Charlie, are you asleep? If you've turned off your phone I don't blame you. Mr. Yu's been telling me that he called Lynn and that she was home all night. He even woke up Claire and asked her where her mother was. She said her mother was home. Then she said they went to the movies. This was after midnight New York time. Mr. Yu is flying out to Singapore. Call me when you wake up." I groaned, did my sit-ups, and got in the shower.

When I'd snapped open a Diet Coke I called Mickey. He said, "Mr. Yu says Claire wouldn't lie."

We discussed the possibilities. Mr. Yu did not actually speak to Lynn. We hated this case. Finally I said, "She leaves for Hong Kong on Wednesday. This is the last thing we'll ever have to do for Mr. Yu. *Finito*."

I hung up and the phone rang and it was Mickey again. "I have to call him back but I'll put him on conference call. I can't talk to him. You talk to him," he said. Mickey dialed Singapore and put himself on Mute; Mr. Yu answered on the first ring. "She go out tonight. He paid for the dinner and now he gets his piece of tail the next night." I gasped silently. "She must spend all day with Alvin. You know—to comfort. He cry, he sorry he send her out. Alvin cry, 'Oh, why I make you do it? Why I make you do it for money like that? Oh, terrible. I feel so bad.' And he cry. And Lynn she comfort him. Then she go out and must sleep with other man for the dinner."

There it was. Mickey was right. Mr. Yu wanted to talk. "Last night. Restaurant. Dinner. Preliminary. She not sleep with him last night. Too soon. Maybe not prepared. Maybe man not prepared. But he spend money and tonight she deliver." He is sure. "He pay for dinner and now get piece of tail." I cringed but was fascinated. "She wear high heels, Mickey say?"

"Yes."

"Describe high heels, please."

I told him that they were under the long dress.

"When she want to excite she wear," he continued. His voice was more highly pitched than usual. "She not wear bra for many years. Wear low-cut dress first time I meet her. I see breasts. I not say anything for three dinners and then I say, 'Don't do this. You not have to do this for me.' She used to not wear bra, now wear uplift pushup to hold up. Lots of underwear now." Pause. "Why she do this? To stimulate, yes?"

"I suppose so. I guess women often dress for seduction," I said rather carefully.

"Yes, yes, yes!" he shouts from Singapore. "It seduction!"

We talked about the car chase. Mickey had said, 'Pretty fancy driving, Charlie,' and I glowed as I thought of it. Mr. Yu wanted details. Poor Mr. Yu. He was spellbound, bewitched by her.

"She go out tonight for sure. So man can get what dinner paid for. She must sleep with him tonight. She owe him. Meanwhile she spend all day with Alvin to comfort. No need to watch for her today. But tonight! Very important!"

All day she flashed into my mind. Lynn with ten cell phones dangling from her curvaceous body, packed into that black sheath with all that underwear. I wondered what she was thinking, doing. Was she drinking wine with a weeping Alvin as he worried about tonight? Was she swearing she didn't mind, was she promising him she wouldn't feel a thing?

Mickey got somebody else to do the Sunday-night stakeout. Lynn was never seen. We decided that maybe the man or client had gone directly upstairs to see her. Extra apartments put to good use.

On Tuesday I flew out of state on another case. I couldn't stall the client any longer and I needed twelve days. Mickey said to go.

The calls from Mr. Yu stopped for a while, and we decided he was busy grinding up rhino horn and gobbling vitamin E in preparation for Lynn's arrival. Mickey faxed a final bill to the Chinese, who said the check was in the mail.

Lynn got on the plane with the nanny and the little girls and arrived safely, and we assumed Lynn spent the night, as promised, in the bed of Mr. Yu. The case was closed, to my great relief.

"I always felt like a voyeur," I said.

Mickey said he felt like a paparazzo. "If it hadn't been given to us by way of that certain law firm, I never would have taken this case."

"It's over," I told him, but he wasn't so sure.

We fell into the rhythm of other cases. I was in the office every day. There were counterfeit cases; the intellectual property lawyers were waiting. Mickey handed me a page with three addresses. "That first one. Watch out. The security in that building is as tight as a clam's ass." I rigged up the video under my clothes trying to figure out which side of a clam would be the rear end then I stepped through the hole in the wall, went out the door, and headed for Broadway.

The faxes started arriving from Singapore again. New addresses to check out. New phone numbers. New bank accounts. More property uncovered.

On Sunday evening Mr. Yu called, then Mickey. I received the news from Singapore and then from Greenwich Village: Lynn would be arriving at Kennedy on Monday. Mickey and I yowled in anguish.

Another stakeout, this time at the International Arrivals Building. Another tail—this time a limo. Another day devoted to the obsession of Mr. Yu. Mickey and I cursed in unison then started to plan. "No wig for me," I told him, "unless the temperature drops below seventy-two."

"Right. I'll tell Mr. Yu." Bailey was barking in the background. "I've got four tags for four possible limos and the flight number and her seat number. Got a crayon?"

Chiefie was on the radio reporting his location and finally we were all in the International Arrivals parking lot looking over at the building. "I invented this uncle who can hardly walk but hates a wheelchair and the Northwest person told me the soonest I can get to him is in the International Arrivals lobby." The clerk had been very helpful. "The possible gates for that flight are 7, 9 and 11, but it doesn't matter because we'll have to wait til she goes through immigration and customs anyway." I wanted to draw the layout on the trunk of the car but there wasn't any dust. Their vehicles were kept in pristine condition. Chiefie and Mickey were smoking these telephone poles and they gave me one. Chiefie lit it for me so I was happy. We had two hours and thirty-eight minutes to wait so we stood around Chiefie's black antenna farm, smoked cigars and discussed logistics.

Time passed, we tossed the cigars. We were ready, the cameras were ready. We moved inside. We waited. I read the *National Enquirer* and Mickey paced around between me and Starbucks.

Alvin met her at the airport. Mickey, Chiefie, and I got pictures and video and tailed the couple back to the apartment. It took all day. Then we headed down Second to a diner in the Fifties. Mickey and I ate like wolves, and Chiefie ordered a fruit salad with cottage cheese and a slice of lemon for his water. In between bites we discussed Mr. Yu.

"We're giving him what he wants," said Chiefie. "Not really but technically."

"It's crummy to think of him putting her on the plane in Hong Kong and then watching a video of her get off the plane in New York falling into the arms of Alvin," I said. I felt sorry for him.

Mickey shrugged. "He evidently read her the riot act when she was in Hong Kong, and it didn't go well. I think he told her to shape up, and she told him to fuck off." He took a bite of London broil. "He was depressed."

I chimed in. "Does he want to keep her under control until his wife dies?"

We didn't know.

"She's using them both. Getting money from Mr. Yu and using it to buy property for herself and Alvin," said Mickey.

"Yeah. All that real estate. That broad's got petty tears all over the place," Chiefie said.

"And Alvin's using her to get money from other men. Both men use her," said Mickey.

Chiefie sighed. "Everybody's using everybody."

I felt a bit sad over my chocolate cake. "I really wanted this to be a love story."

The two investigators looked at me then at each other and raised their eyebrows. I raised my shoulders and let them drop. We all started eating again.

My photos and the men's videos were sent off to Hong Kong. The final bill was faxed to Singapore and it was paid.

I was in and out of the office reading files, to and from locations on Broadway. Mickey was usually on the phone with lawyers, with clients. Other cases were crowding out the saga of Mr. Yu but Mickey still left messages on my machine with a pretty fair imitation of his voice. The summer was over.

One rainy September afternoon, in the office, Mickey said, "You know, Charlie, it was all for the former father-in-law." I put down the pages I was reading, and he went on. "Mr. Yu showed him the videos of the way the kids are being brought up."

"The former father-in-law who is still and always will be the grandfather," I mused. I remembered that first day when he told us the family of the dead husband still paid for some of her phone bills. "But how can Mr. Yu, the lover of Lynn, go to this man and . . ." Suddenly I realized as Mickey said it.

"Because Mr. Yu is the godfather of Claire." Mickey turned in his chair to face me. There was a gleam in his eye.

So there it was. Mr. Yu, in his relentless struggle to have Lynn for himself, had hired us to help him persuade the grandfather to exile Alvin, that unsuitable foreigner, from his grandchildren's life. This meant Mr. Yu could again be with Lynn—as lover, protector, and companion with "dip pockets."

Boundless was the passion of Mr. Yu for the hooker from Hong Kong.

CPSIA information can be obtained
at www.ICGtesting.com
Printed in the USA
FFHW022251270219
50752012-56154FF